CARYL CHURCHILL

Elaine Aston

Third Edition

NORTHCOTE

BRITISH COUNCIL

by Northcote House Publishers Ltd, Horndon House, Horndon, Tavistock, Devon, PL19 9NQ, United Kingdom.
Tel: +44 (01822) 810066 Fax: +44 (01822) 810034.

British Library Cataloguing-in-Publication Data
A catalogue record for this book is available from the British Library

ISBN 978-0-7463-1208-7

Typeset by PDQ Typesetting, Newcastle-under-Lyme
Printed and bound in the United Kingdom

for Ian,
Magdalene and Daniel

Contents

Acknowledgements

I should like to thank Methuen and Nick Hern Books, the publishers of Caryl Churchill's works, whose excellent editions I used in writing this study. I am grateful to the University of Nitra, Slovakia, for permission to reproduce the commentary on *Blue Heart*, originally published as part of the conference proceedings on 'Intertextuality and the Postmodern' (Nitra, 1999). Thanks also to Nick Hern and Guy Chapman who generously shared early information about the script and production details of *Hotel*, and to Nick Hern again for sending me the script of *Far Away*. I am grateful to Mel Kenyon and Kirsty Coombs at Casarotto Ramsay & Associates for always being willing to help with Churchillian enquiries. To my dear friend and Churchill scholar Janelle Reinelt, a thank you for your insightful thoughts and company at the *Light Shining in Buckinghamshire* revival in 1997. My thanks also go to R. Darren Gobert for his generous sharing of bibliographical materials. Finally, a special thank you to Caryl Churchill without whose outstanding work in the theatre this study, now in its third edition, would not have been possible.

Biographical Outline

1938 Churchill born in London. Early childhood spent in and near London, with exception of short time spent in Lake District during war years.

1948 Just before age of 10, family move to Canada and live in Montreal until Churchill nearly 17.

1957–60 Student years at Lady Margaret Hall, Oxford. Student productions of *Downstairs* (1958), which went to NUS festival, and *Having a Wonderful Time* (1960), Questors Theatre, London.

1961 Student production of play for voices, *You've No Need to be Frightened*. Marriage to barrister David Harter.

1962 *Easy Death*, amateur production, Oxford Experimental Theatre Club, Oxford Playhouse. *The Ants*, first professional radio play, broadcast.

1963–9 Birth of three sons. Period of being at home with young children becomes politicizing experience. Churchill continues writing for radio: *Lovesick* (1967) and *Identical Twins* (1968) broadcast.

1971 Radio plays *Abortive* and *Not Not Not Not Not Enough Oxygen* broadcast.

1972 Radio plays *Schreber's Nervous Illness* and *Henry's Past* broadcast. Around time of *Schreber*, writes unperformed play *The Hospital at the Time of the Revolution*. *The Judge's Wife* broadcast on BBC television. First professional stage production, *Owners*, Royal Court Theatre Upstairs, London. *Schreber* given stage performance at King's Head Theatre, London.

1973 Radio play *Perfect Happiness* broadcast. *Owners* premièred in New York.

1974 *Turkish Delight* broadcast on BBC television. First woman writer in residence at Royal Court Theatre.

1975   *Save it for the Minister*, with Mary O'Malley and Cherry Potter, broadcast on BBC television. Association with Royal Court continues with staging of *Objections to Sex and Violence* and *Moving Clocks Go Slow* (Theatre Upstairs). *Perfect Happiness* given a stage performance at Soho Poly, London.

1976   Begins working with companies: Joint Stock and Monstrous Regiment. *Light Shining in Buckinghamshire* performed at Traverse Theatre, Edinburgh; on tour, and at Royal Court Theatre Upstairs, London. Begins long association with director Max Stafford-Clark. *Vinegar Tom* performed at Humberside Theatre, Hull; on tour, and at ICA and Half Moon theatres, London.

1977   *Traps* performed at Royal Court Theatre Upstairs, London. Contributes to *Floorshow*, a touring cabaret, scripted with Bryony Lavery, Michelene Wandor and David Bradford.

1978   *The After-Dinner Joke* and *The Legion Hall Bombing* (censored version) broadcast on BBC television. Writes play *Seagulls* (not performed until 2002).

1979   Joint Stock production of *Cloud Nine* staged at Dartington College of Arts; on tour, and Royal Court Theatre, London.

1980   *Three More Sleepless Nights* staged at Soho Poly and Royal Court Theatre Upstairs, London.

1981   *Cloud Nine* premièred in New York.

1982   *Crimes* broadcast on television. *Top Girls*, staged at Royal Court Theatre, London, and subsequently transferred to New York. *Cloud Nine* wins Obie award.

1983   *Fen*, Joint Stock production, staged at University of Essex Theatre, Colchester; Almeida and Royal Court Theatres, London, and transferred to New York. *Top Girls* wins Obie award.

1984   *Softcops*, originally written in 1978, is given its first performance by the RSC at the Barbican Pit, London. Churchill contributes to a performance art production, *Midday Sun*, ICA, London, which marks her growing interest in non-text-based theatre. Winner of Susan Smith Blackburn prize for *Fen*.

1985   First Methuen collection of plays published.

1986   *A Mouthful of Birds*, a Joint Stock production, co-written with David Lan, performed at Birmingham Repertory Theatre; on tour, and Royal Court Theatre, London. Production gives Churchill the opportunity of working with choreographer Ian Spink.

1987   *Serious Money* performed at Royal Court Theatre, London. Transfer to Wyndham's, London, and later to New York. Wins several theatre awards including a second Susan Smith Blackburn Award.

1988   Works again with Spink on *Fugue*, a dance-based piece, broadcast on Channel 4 television. *Serious Money* plays Broadway. *The Caryl Churchill Omnibus* broadcast on BBC television.

1989   *Icecream* staged at Royal Court Theatre, London. Churchill writes companion piece *Hot Fudge*, performed at Royal Court Theatre Upstairs, London.

1990   Churchill goes to Romania with drama students from Central School of Speech and Drama. Writes *Mad Forest*, 'a play from Romania', performed at Central and Royal Court Theatre, London, and National Theatre, Bucharest. Second Methuen collection of plays and *Churchill: Shorts* (Nick Hern) anthology published.

1991   *Lives of the Great Poisoners*, with Ian Spink and Orlando Gough, performed at Arnolfini, Bristol; on tour, and Riverside Studios, London. *Top Girls* broadcast on BBC television.

1994   *The Skriker* staged at the Cottesloe, Royal National Theatre, London. Translates *Thyestes*, staged at Royal Court Theatre Upstairs, London.

1997   *Hotel* performed by Second Stride at the Place Theatre, London. *This is a Chair* staged by the Royal Court at the Duke of York's, London. *Blue Heart* performed by Out of Joint, Theatre Royal, Bury St Edmunds; Traverse Theatre, Edinburgh, and Royal Court, Duke of York's.

1998   Third collection of plays published by Nick Hern.

2000   *Far Away* opens at Royal Court, Sloane Square, London.

2001   West End transfer of *Far Away* to the Albery Theatre, London.

2002   *A Number* staged at the Royal Court Theatre Downstairs, London, in tandem with a series of 'Caryl Churchill Events': rehearsed readings of select early works – *Seagulls, Three More Sleepless Nights, Moving Clocks Go Slow* and *Owners* – productions without décor of *This is a Chair, Not Not Not Not Not Enough Oxygen* and *Identical Twins. A Number* wins Evening Standard Award for Best New Play. *Far Away* premières in New York. Churchill writes short text, 'She bit her tongue', for *Plants and Ghosts*, Siobhan Davies Dance Company, performed in USAF Air Force Base, Upper Heyford, Oxfordshire.

2003   *A Number* transfers to Albery Theatre, West End, London.

2004   Churchill contributes to 'War Correspondence' at the Royal Court, London. *A Number* opens at New York Theater Workshop.

2005   *A Dream Play* (Strindberg) new version by Churchill, staged at Cottesloe, Royal National Theatre, London.

2006   *Drunk Enough to Say I Love You?* staged in Royal Court Theatre Downstairs, London. Churchill writes libretto for Orlando Gough's *We Turned on the Light*, performed at BBC proms.

2008   Translates Olivier Choinière's *Bliss (Félicité)*, staged at the Royal Court Theatre Upstairs, London. Royal Court hosts Churchill's seventieth birthday celebrations – ten playwrights direct their favourite Churchill play: *Owners* (April de Angelis); *Light Shining* (Mark Ravenhill); *Vinegar Tom* (Winsome Pinnock); *Top Girls* (Nicholas Wright); *Three More Sleepless Nights* (debbie tucker green); *Icecream* (Wallace Shawn); *The Skriker* (Zinnie Harris); *Blue Heart* (Marius von Mayenburg); *Far Away* (Martin Crimp) and *A Number* (Joe Penhall). *Drunk Enough to Say I Love You?* has American première at The Public Theater, New York and *Top Girls* has New York revival. Fourth collection of plays published by Nick Hern. *A Number* filmed for television by HBO and BBC.

2009   *Seven Jewish Children*, Churchill's 'play for Gaza', performed at Royal Court Theatre Downstairs, London.

Abbreviations

The two Methuen volumes of Churchill plays *Churchill: Plays One* and *Churchill: Plays Two* (London, 1985 and 1990) have been used throughout, cited in the text as *P1* and *P2* respectively, followed by the page number. The collection of short plays *Churchill: Shorts* (London: Hern, 1990) is abbreviated to *S*. Full details of the plays contained in these volumes can be found in the Select Bibliography.

Abbreviations for single plays are as follows:

**BH	*Blue Heart*
**DE	*Drunk Enough to Say I Love You?*
**FA	*Far Away*
**H	*Hotel*
*IC	*Icecream*
*LGP	*Lives of the Great Poisoners*
*MB	*A Mouthful of Birds*
*MF	*Mad Forest*
**N	*A Number*
OSV	*Objections to Sex and Violence*
SJC	*Seven Jewish Children*
**TC	*This is a Chair*
*TS	*The Skriker*

*Have since been published with *Thyestes* in *Churchill: Plays Three* (London: Nick Hern, 1998)

**Also available with *A Dream Play* in *Caryl Churchill – Plays: 4* (London: Nick Hern, 2008)

Preface

This is the third edition of *Caryl Churchill* for the series Writers and their Work. First published in 1997, the original monograph set out to provide a critically informed and accessible approach to Churchill's playwriting from the early years through to the 1994 production of *The Skriker*. Chapters one to five constitute the text of the first edition: a survey of Churchill's early writing for radio, television and theatre (Chapter 1); the importance of Churchill's theatre to contemporary women's drama and feminist theatre scholarship (Chapter 2); the socialist canvas of her playwriting (Chapter 3); the representation of oppressed communities (Chapter 4); and her 'shapeshifting', experimental approaches to writing for theatre and performance (Chapter 5). In 2001 Northcote House published a second, updated edition of the study for which I wrote Chapter 6 which gives an account of Churchill's work from 1997 through to the production of *Far Away* in 2000. Chapter 7, written for this 2010 third edition, catches up with Churchill; details her most recent plays at the Royal Court Theatre, London.

   In 2008 Caryl Churchill celebrated her seventieth birthday – a celebration she shared with the Royal Court, the theatre with which she has been most closely associated since its staging of *Owners* in the Upstairs studio space back in 1972. Fêted as one of the most formally innovative and politically incisive dramatists writing for the contemporary stage, Churchill's capacity for theatrical invention and political intervention remains undiminished. While her socialist dream of a 'decentralized, nonauthoritarian' society now seems an increasingly remote, 'far away', possibility, Churchill remains fiercely opposed, as her theatre attests, to the nightmarish intensification, rather than diminution, of capitalist greed, violence, terror and damage that Churchillian landscapes now point to as occurring on a global scale. Her's is a radical theatre voice, steadfast in its creative and political address of the dangerous consequences of a failure to believe in and to realize more egalitarian and less damaged futures. The words of Churchill's Nell, the most outspoken, radical, female protestor in *Fen* and, like Churchill, an accomplished teller of 'frightening' stories, seem apposite – 'I won't turn back for you or anyone'.

1

Beginnings: Radio, Stage and Television

> [I know] quite well what kind of society I would like: decentralized, nonauthoritarian, communist, nonsexist – a society in which people can be in touch with their feelings, and in control of their lives. But it always sounds both ridiculous and unattainable when you put it into words.[1]

Caryl Churchill has been performing her radical, revisionist view of society for over thirty years in professional theatre and is now acknowledged as one of the foremost, innovative writers for the contemporary stage.

She began to write as a young girl, producing mostly short stories and poems. When asked in interview whether she started to write 'because of a love of words' Churchill observed of herself:

> I don't know. That must be part of it. The fact that I was an only child may have helped. I had friends, but I did have quite a lot of time when I could be alone. Planning stories would be like solitary playing. I would invent a lot of characters, and descriptions of where they lived and maps, and it would be a whole game. So there was that sort of overlap. I also had a very close friend and we used to play a game which, looking back, reached a point where it was more like improvising plays.[2]

One recollection she offered with certainty, however, was her early interest in the theatre:

> I was also separately interested in the theatre. I liked going to plays. I used to want there to be plays done at school, and there weren't. When I was fifteen, I went off to a summer theatre in Canada, outside Montreal, and painted scenery. I didn't really put the two things together till a few years after that, at university.[3]

During her childhood in the 1940s, which was spent largely in London, and her teenage years in the 1950s, by which time the family had relocated to Montreal, Canada, Churchill recollects listening to the radio rather than watching television. Her writing as a young adult reflects the influence of this medium. Among her early works, for example, is the play for voices, *You've No Need to be Frightened* written in 1959 during Churchill's university years (1957–60), spent back in England at Lady Margaret Hall, Oxford. Her first professional production, *The Ants* (1962), although written with television in mind was, on the advice of her agent, Margaret Ramsay, put forward for radio broadcasting (*P1* xi).

While linking her attraction to radio to the pleasure she derived from this medium in her formative years,[4] it is also significant that the solitary career of radio dramatist was one which Churchill was able to combine with her career as a mother of three sons, born between 1963 and 1969. In her own mother, Churchill had an example of a woman combining work with family life:

> She started out her life adventurously, leaving school at fourteen, working in an office, becoming a secretary and then a model ...There are wonderful photos of her saying, 'I'm so tired, but thanks to Ovaltine...' Later she began to get bit parts in films, and she went on with it after I was born, only stopping because of the war. I mostly remember my mother at home, but she did talk to me about working, and the fact that she used not to wear her wedding ring to work. I had the feeling, rather early on, that having a career was in no way incompatible with staying married and being very happy.[5]

Later, the issue of women, families and work would be debated and taken up by Churchill in the politics of major plays such as *Top Girls* and *Fen*.

Meanwhile, Churchill also began to write for stage and television. In her father, a cartoonist by profession, she had contact with someone who was working in images, although it was only later, she confesses, that she began to make connections between their respective crafts: 'Cartoons are really so much like plays. An image with somebody saying something'.[6] She recollects writing about 'ten other plays' for theatre and television during the 1960s and early 1970s (*P1* xi).[7]

4

Although she continued to write for television until 1982 when *Crimes* was broadcast, and returned briefly to the medium in 1988 for her dance-drama collaboration *Fugue*, the 1970s might be seen as a phasing out of her interest in television work. On the other hand, writing for the stage was to become increasingly important during this decade of her artistic career.

Churchill's early work reflects a number of the stylistic and thematic concerns of her later stage plays. Experimenting with traditional approaches to dramatic writing, playing with the conventions of form, time, narrative, structure, language and dialogue are stylistically evident in the early dramas. In the radio plays, the power structures of marital and familial relations are thematized in *The Ants* (1962), *Lovesick* (1967), *Abortive* (1971), *Henry's Past* (1972) and *Perfect Happiness* (1973); identity in crisis is presented in *Identical Twins* (1968) and the schizophrenic world of *Schreber's Nervous Illness* (1972), and 'madness . . . sweeping the country' in a world starved of natural resources is depicted in *Not Not Not Not Not Enough Oxygen* (1971). The unperformed stage play *The Hospital at the Time of the Revolution*, written at the same time as *Schreber's Nervous Illness*, again looks at madness, but in the specific context of colonial war, and Churchill's early play for television *The Judge's Wife* (1972) questions reactionary politics with revolutionary action.

Rather than survey all of this early work, this chapter will focus on a cross-section of writing for radio, stage and television. The selection is designed to illustrate Churchill's early preoccupation with 'madness and civilization', and explores her critique of the regulating systems of authority which determine 'normal' behaviour, and, conversely, marginalize and police the 'abnormal', sexually 'deviant', 'insane' or 'criminal', and so on. Although this work dates from the mid-1960s to the early 1970s, the gender politics (and racial politics in *The Hospital*) stage a number of issues pertinent to current feminist theorizings of sexuality, power, subjectivity, cultural identity and the (de-)construction of gender.

'LOVE'S CURE': *LOVESICK*

Lovesick, Churchill's second professionally broadcast radio play (1967), focuses on the attempts of a psychiatrist, Dr Hodge, to 'cure' or 'correct' the 'deviant' desires of his patients and friends through aversion therapy. Aversion therapy was a form of medical treatment in which patients were administered nausea-inducing drugs and were confronted with images of their 'abnormal' desires. In theory, a patient would be 'cured' of his or her 'lovesickness' as he or she learnt to associate a 'deviant' desire with the nausea and vomiting. In the radio play, for example, Hodge describes how he successfully 'cured' a 'dowdy nymphomaniac':

> First she was given a drug which causes nausea and then photographs of naked men. I wasn't sure if photographs would be enough so at a later stage I put my extraordinarily unquestioning and really stupid assistant Jenks into her room and told him to undress. To my delight she vomited repeatedly. (S 10–11)

In the 1950s, aversion therapy was especially used to 'cure' homosexual patients of their 'perverse' desires, a practice which Churchill critiques in the radio play when a homosexual 'cure' goes wrong and ends in suicide.

The narrative thread of *Lovesick* involves a complex weaving of 'illicit' relationships. Through Jessica Zolotov, who is having an affair with Hodge's friend Max, married to Lucy, Hodge is introduced to Ellen McNab. While working on a 'cure' for Ellen's alcoholic aunt, he becomes obsessed with Ellen. Although married, Ellen desires Kevin, one of Jessica's two sons, while Kevin is interested in starting a homosexual relationship. Like a modern Racinian tragedy, the chain of unrequited desires is further complicated by Jessica's feigned interest in Max as a means of countering her incestuous relationship with her other son, Robert. Ultimately, Hodge attempts to 'cure' Kevin of his homosexuality, and to treat Ellen's desire for Kevin and her phobia of him. His designs are thwarted by Robert, who intervenes and deceives Hodge's assistant into reversing instructions so that Ellen has Kevin's cure, is disgusted by men and falls in love with her female nurse, and Kevin, with Ellen's cure, hates himself but is desperately in love with Hodge.

Hodge functions as the key narrative voice. The act of narration reverses his empowered position as psychiatrist and places him in the disempowered role of patient. As confessor, story-teller, it is Hodge who is in the psychiatrist's chair, and the radio audience who is positioned as 'doctor' hearing the confessed narrative. This technique of role reversal is central to Churchill's critique of the policing of desire. It calls into question the criteria of sexual behaviour by which the white, middle-class, male psychiatrist – now positioned as patient – judges 'normalcy'. Hodge's 'cure' of the rapist and murderer, for example, 'privately' told to the listening audience, or doctor, takes on the tone of a 'criminal' confession:

> Another remarkable cure was Smith, the rapist and murderer. The papers were full of his mutilated victims but to my joy he came to me before the police knew anything about him. Max wanted me to castrate him but my usual method was perfectly successful, leaving only a slight distaste for sex and butchers in an otherwise well-balanced personality. He is back at work, the joy, as always, of his old parents, and my only worry is that the police may yet catch him and hold him responsible for his corpses. (S 11)

Moreover, Hodge's attempt to 'cure' Kevin of his homosexuality and Kevin's subsequent suicide highlight the dangers of regulating sexuality. Hodge's own heterosexual position is further undermined as he confesses to a suppression of homosexual desire:

> I [Hodge] might have persuaded him [Kevin] to have treatment, he loved me enough to do anything for me. More than anyone else has ever done. But I was too disheartened to start again at once and he killed himself before I got down to it...I've homosexual tendencies like anyone else, but well suppressed, and it was most inconvenient to have them stirred. (S 18)

Ultimately, the characters liberate themselves into sexually 'transgressive' positions: Ellen finds a lesbian relationship with her nurse; Jessica remains in a relationship with her son Robert; and Max returns to his wife, Lucy, in a role-reversal relationship where Lucy goes out to work in 'trouser suits' and Max stays at home and feels comfortable in 'wearing her [Lucy's] pink silk dress and blue toque' (S 17). Conversely, it is Hodge who is left in need of treatment. As the play ends, he prepares, hesitantly, to apply aversive therapy to his own heterosexual ('normal') desires for Ellen:

> I have a photograph of Ellen on my desk. I've plenty more, and I will take the drug in just a minute. It can't be fear of nausea that makes

7

me hesitate. By next week, if I don't turn back, I could be free to concentrate on my work, with no thought of Ellen, whose beauty is great. (S 19)

The isolation of the heterosexual male in a group of repressed sexual 'deviants', whose forbidden desires surface through aversion to prescriptive heterosexual role play, is a model which Churchill would later use in the writing of *Cloud Nine*.

'THE FEMALE MALADY': *SCHREBER'S NERVOUS ILLNESS*

In contrast to *Lovesick*, *Schreber's Nervous Illness*, broadcast on radio in 1972, presents the narrative viewpoint of the schizophrenic patient, Daniel Paul Schreber. Schreber was the subject of one of Freud's case studies, written shortly before Schreber's death in 1911.[8] Churchill's source material was Schreber's memoirs, first published in 1903, and translated in 1955 as *Memoirs of My Nervous Illness* (S 58).

Schreber is set in asylums in Leipzig and Dresden around the turn of the century. The voice of Schreber's psychiatrist, Dr Weber, punctuates Schreber's narrative of madness with clinical diagnoses, descriptions of the patient's behaviour, symptoms, and so on. Significant in Schreber's narrative is the descent into madness of a man who was a high-status, authority figure; a former president of the Court of Appeal in Dresden. However, he works through the paranoid delusions of his first breakdown in which he saw his doctor, Professor Flechsig, as persecutor, as 'soul murderer', and comes to terms with the divine sufferings he believes he experiences through his body, which he hears as voices or 'rays', in a bid to be discharged from the asylum. Ironically, it is to the Appeal Court of which he was once the president that he has to make his application for freedom, which is finally granted. Schreber's comment on his starting life outside of the asylum again challenges the definition of what is judged to be 'sane' or 'mad'. Describing his need to control his 'bellowing' in public, one of the remaining symptoms of his illness, Schreber concludes:

> While going for walks along country roads or in fields I make things easy for myself and simply let the bellowing happen. Sometimes it continues for five or ten minutes, during which time I feel perfectly

well. Anyone who saw me would, however, hardly understand what I was doing, and might really think he was seeing a madman. (S 93)

That Weber makes brief comments on or offers explanations for Schreber's condition, but is not heard conversing or communicating with Schreber directly, is significant in the context of the radio play's social and cultural production. The 1960s witnessed a rebellion against traditional methods of psychiatry: a rejection of shock treatments, ECT, the isolated institutionalization of patients, and so on. The publication of R. D. Laing's influential study of *The Divided Self* (1960) was, for a time, a controversial but seminal reference point calling for a different approach to psychiatric care – one based on close communication between patient and doctor; on dialogue rather than clinical diagnosis. Laing's work influenced a number of writers, among them playwrights David Mercer, who wrote the television play *In Two Minds* (1967), which was later made into a film, and David Edgar, who used the contemporary case study of one of Laing's patients for his stage play *Mary Barnes* (1977). Churchill's radio play may, therefore, be seen as part of the contemporary debate on schizophrenia. Her play, however, differs from the other two examples in so far as it uses the turn-of-the-century memoirs to treat a contemporary issue in dramatic form, rather than making use of modern case studies. Interrogating the present through staging a (historical) past is a strategy central to several of Churchill's subsequent stage plays.

Looking at *Schreber* through a modern feminist framework of approaches to psychiatry and psychoanalysis makes the 'unmanning' of Schreber's body – his description of a resistance to, but gradual acceptance of a process of feminization – of particular interest. In the field of French feminist theory and psychoanalytic writing, for example, Hélène Cixous's *l'écriture féminine* examines the binary opposition of Woman as Other than man, and calls for women to struggle against 'conventional man' in order to write themselves into being.[9] In her radio play, Churchill uses the body of the 'conventional man' to 'write', or rather to stage, the feminine Other. Critic Amelia Howe Kritzer develops this point by applying Elaine Showalter's concept of 'the female malady' – based on the binary opposition between rationality/masculinity and madness/femininity – to her analysis of *Schreber*.[10] Kritzer explains:

Churchill uses as her main character a man afflicted with the 'female malady' of madness, rather than a woman reacting madly to the world of male-imposed structures. In taking an approach that defies habitual divisions and avoids reinforcing such division, Churchill emphasizes that any individual – male or female – may be both a perpetrator and a victim of patriarchal oppression. At the same time, Schreber's story, as presented in this radio play, gives a compelling capsulization of the relation of women to patriarchal power.[11]

Hence, like Hodge, who is doctor and patient, Schreber the erstwhile judge and patriarch encodes masculinity and power; Schreber the patient embodies femininity and disempowerment.

Schreber's contact with the feminine Other is experienced not through logos (speech), which he uses in his madness to rationalize an exclusion of the feminine, but through the body as he imagines his physical transformation from man to woman:

> I am preoccupied with changing into a woman...Now the voluptuousness was so great that some rays began to like entering my body. I considered it my right and duty to cultivate feelings of voluptuousness. Few people have been brought up according to such strict moral principles as I or practised such moderation in matters of sex. But to attract the rays I must image myself as man and woman in one person having intercourse with myself. (S 78)

The possibility of moving beyond the gender divide lies in the androgynous play of Schreber's madness. It is significant, however, that the possibility of 'voluptuousness', or the potential for what Cixous might call in her writing *jouissance* (total joy or ecstasy), can only be expressed in the space of the asylum. In the real, 'sane' world, into which 'conventional man' is returned, the binary order of masculine versus feminine is not to be transgressed. When, like Max in *Lovesickness*, Schreber takes pleasure in dressing his body in signs of conventional femininity, and describes 'standing in front of the mirror with ribbons and cheap necklaces on my body', he admits that this is 'the only thing that could be considered unreasonable' by the ('sane') world outside the asylum (S 88). Repression of the feminine is necessary for Schreber to secure his release. As he 'rationalizes' in his state of madness, 'nothing can exist permanently which is against the Order of the World' (S 80–1). The dis-orderly world of theatre can, however, make visible utopian possibilities of gender play, as Churchill would further show in the cross-dressing strategies of

Cloud Nine or the androgynous playing in *A Mouthful of Birds.*

'BLACK SKINS, WHITE MASKS': *THE HOSPITAL AT THE TIME OF THE REVOLUTION*

Written at the time of *Schreber*, *The Hospital* is an unstaged play which also examines madness. The action is set in 1956 in the Blida-Joinville Hospital in Algeria during the Algerian war. The central protagonist is Frantz Fanon who was head of the psychiatric unit at Blida-Joinville, a position he later resigned from to join in the War of National Liberation fought by the Algerian people. Fanon's writing on the links between mental disorders and colonial war was a key source for the *Hospital*, and details extracted from his case studies are woven into Churchill's dramatization.[12]

For example, Churchill's three Algerian patients, referred to as A, B, and C, are drawn from Fanon's series of patient case studies which detail different psychotic reactions and disorders as a result of war, specifically colonial war. Patient A suffers from the delayed shock of having been responsible for killing a number of people in the bombing of a bar. B is a torture victim who tries to hang himself in the hospital when he sees his torturer – a European police inspector who has been admitted as a patient to the hospital, but whom B, in his state of trauma, believes has come to torture him again. Patient C is a light-skinned Algerian who is paranoid that everyone mistakes him for a European and believes him to be a coward and traitor of his Algerian people:

> I've never been interested in politics, only in engineering, and there's nothing wrong with that. You wouldn't say I was a European would you? I've a pale skin but that's from being ill and indoors so much. You wouldn't say I was a European? To look at me you'd see I was an Algerian, wouldn't you, just by looking at me. (*S* 120)

The colonial issue of 'Black Skins, White Masks'[13] is not only a thematic concern in *The Hospital*, but race also informs Churchill's techniques of theatricalization. For the staging and costuming she instructs that the 'black skins' of the Algerians be set in the 'bare white walls' of the hospital (*S* 97). Medicine, the

11

hospital, is associated with Western 'civilization'; the 'sick' Algerians are there to be 'cured', colonized by the West. Fanon, as a Black doctor from Martinique who trained in Paris, signs the schizophrenic split of colonizer and colonized on and through the white (European) uniform of medicine on his Black skin. As a doctor, he has to treat both the white colonizers, stressed and traumatized by the acts of torture they carry out, and their Black victims.

In addition to the writings of Fanon, Churchill also acknowledges a debt to R. D. Laing as a source for *The Hospital* (S 96). Churchill's interest in Laing can be most obviously traced in the dramatization of Françoise, daughter of the '*middle-aged Europeans*' Monsieur and Madame (S 97). Françoise is brought by her parents to Fanon for treatment of a behavioural disorder which Fanon subsequently diagnoses as schizophrenia. Françoise's illness is identified by her parents as the progressive degeneration of a 'good' daughter who turns 'bad'; whose actions become so increasingly abnormal that she has to be 'mad'. This is a pattern which Laing discusses in his case study of Julie and which he attributes in part to the infantilization of the child which hinders the autonomy, or sense of self, in the adolescent adult.[14] Françoise is similarly infantilized by her parents, particularly her mother, and Churchill writes this on to her body in the direction '*she is neatly and prettily dressed in a style rather too young*' (S 97).

However, Françoise's case is further complicated by the colonial war. Her father, the colonizer, tortures his victims in their home and Françoise hears their screams in the night: 'My mother has killed a little girl. But no one punishes her, do they? My father has killed far more people. I can't give you a list of the names but I hear the screams all night' (S 113–14). The 'sick' or 'murdered' daughter of the colonial oppressors mirrors the position of the colonized – a loss of self, identity, culture and race due to the violent imposition of white, Western values. Infantilization and colonialization are explicitly linked as the parents attempt to police the 'bad' child by keeping her locked up, just like the 'natives' who are brought in for questioning. The starved body Françoise believes to be poisoned by her mother, and which she sees as already dead, is also a body poisoned and murdered by the colonial war. Starving the body expresses her guilt as a 'sick' daughter of the West.[15] The final scene is of Fanon and Françoise, sitting first in silence, and then Françoise trying to explain her absent body to Fanon:

> Under the dress I can't find where I am. So when I take it off there's nobody there. They can't see Françoise because she was taken off upstairs and nobody came downstairs and into the room. My mother made that dress to kill me. It ate me away. That was a poison dress I put on. (S 146)

The 'frightening' future for the disempowered daughter in the patriarchal, capitalist, colonizing systems of the West, is an issue which Churchill raises in later plays – most obviously represented in the figure of Angie in *Top Girls*.

CRIME AND PUNISHMENT: *THE JUDGE'S WIFE*

The Judge's Wife, Churchill's first drama to be broadcast on television (1972), reflects a shift from the psychiatric and psychoanalytic questions of 'madness and civilization' in medicine, to the political and existential questions of autonomy, law, order and 'civilized' behaviour in the legal system. The Judge, who is designated by title and role, rather than represented as an individual, named person, is the 'conventional man' of authority Schreber presumably once was. Crime and punishment are problematized in the play, which opens with the shooting of the Judge by Michael Warren, brother of a revolutionary 'criminal' Vernon Warren, whom the Judge has sentenced to a heavy prison term. Who is the criminal? Is the Judge's sentencing of Vernon Warren 'criminal'? Are the nonspecified violent revolutionary acts of Vernon Warren criminal or just? Is the shooting of the Judge a crime or suitable punishment for the act of sentencing? The shooting of the Judge is played and re-played in the drama, while events leading up to the shooting are dramatized through domestic scenes in the Judge's household between the Judge, his wife Caroline, her sister Barbara, and the maid, Peg.

As in *The Hospital*, power is encoded in vestimentary signs of authority: the white coat of the doctor, the robes of the judge. When these are removed, as, for example, in a domestic scene when the Judge is seen preparing for a bath with the help of his subservient wife, then the reality of the powerless *'naked, fat, old, defenceless, body'* is exposed (*S* 150). Identity is therefore at risk when people fail to recognize, or reject and rebel against the authority signed on the public body. As the Judge explains to his wife with regard to Warren, 'I was trying my right to exist' (*S* 156). It is only by playing out the role of judiciary to an extreme that the Judge feels able to exist. As in Jean Genet's theatre, in plays such as *The Blacks* or *The Maids*, if you represent authority you play authority until it is played out. If you are cast in the role of the enemy, then you have the freedom to play the enemy to a violent extreme, until the role is unmasked. The repeated, ritualized death of the Judge is a playing out, critique and destruction of the authority which constitutes his identity. In a monologue delivered in the presence of her sister Barbara after the 'death' of her husband, Caroline rationalizes his death as follows:

> He had become the enemy. He loathed himself. He said he would commit suicide. And then at a brilliant stroke he saw what he could do for other people. He could be the enemy...He could live out his way of life but more extremely...He could use his power unjustly so that someone would be forced to take it away from him. (*S* 162)

When she speaks, however, she speaks, as the title of the play indicates, as the Judge's wife. In the private, domestic sphere, she is seen in her role as the subservient wife. At a mirror in the bedroom, she is shown trying out a smiling mask. Its artificiality is exposed as she tries on the smile and lets it slip. Only after the 'death' of her husband does she move beyond the public gaze of the mirror when she appears alongside her sister in a *'dressing-gown'*, with *'her hair...unbrushed, her face crumpled'* (*S* 161). Now her sister is her mirror: *'they are two old women'* (*S* 161). In narrating and rationalizing her husband's death she finally plays out her own role as the Judge's wife. The disempowerment of the women characters, especially the Irish maid who rebels against her imperialist, English 'master' by leaving her employment, raises gender oppression as an issue in the use and abuse of power.

The crime and punishment narrative in *The Judge's Wife* is dramatized in a non-naturalistic style. The repeated flashbacks of the shooting disrupt narrative linearity and chronology.

Identity is unfixed in the doubling of roles as one actor plays both Michael and Vernon Warren, a device which poses the question – who really kills the Judge? Scenes from outside the courtroom, a public sphere, are meta-theatrically represented on a television screen in the Judge's bedroom, a private space, and so on. In short, this early television play is replete with techniques of destabilization which are precursors of theatrical devices Churchill subsequently develops in her theatre. Although Patrick Campbell, reviewing for *Stage and Television Today* was critical of the play for being 'one of those plays which leave the critic with a strong sense of frustration, seeing so much originality just failing in the event to fulfil its promise',[17] it is the 'promise' of things to come which, retrospectively, strikes the reader and viewer. From this point of view, *The Judge's Wife* illustrates Churchill's early preoccupation with finding innovative forms to work in (a point taken up and pursued in Chapter 5 of this study). As Churchill herself explains:

> I do enjoy the form of things. I enjoy finding the form that seems best to fit what I'm thinking about. I don't set out to find a bizarre way of writing. I certainly don't think that you have to force it. But, on the whole, I enjoy plays that are non naturalistic and don't move at real time.[18]

As a selection of Churchill's early writings was not widely available until the publication of the anthology *Shorts* in 1990, the 'beginnings' of her writing career have not, as yet, received all the critical interest due to them from women's studies. While, for example, Cixous's stage play *Portrait of Dora* (1979), which re-stages Freud's case study of Dora and undermines the traditional power relations between the empowered psychiatrist and disempowered female patient, has received much feminist critical attention, Churchill's en-gendered explorations of 'madness and civilization', as discussed here, have not.

Elsewhere I have argued that women's studies may find a valuable source of critical practice in the form of feminist theatre: a medium which makes visible its theoretical and critical concerns on and through the body.[19] I would want to argue that Churchill's staging of the body in her early work, whether this is the 'cured', 'unmanned', 'feminine' or 'colonized' body of the oppressed, or the representation of

15

2

The 'Woman Writer'

In 1977 Ann McFerran conducted an interview for *Time Out* with nine British women playwrights, and headed the commentaries with the statement 'the male-dominated theatre is giving way (somewhat)'.[1] In retrospect, our 'male-dominated theatre' hardly seems to have given way at all, but those women in touch with the Second Women's Liberation Movement in the 1970s were, in the climate of feminism, able to view the possibility of a more equitable future with a degree of optimism. Gillian Hanna, a founding company member of Monstrous Regiment, with whom Churchill worked on *Vinegar Tom* (1976) and the *Floorshow* cabaret (1977), recollects:

> Feminism was leaping in our heads...To be a woman in 1975 and not to have felt the excitement of things starting to change, possibilities in the air, would have meant that you were only half alive...
>
> ...we wanted to change the world. At the time, this didn't seem like such an outrageous project. All around us, women in every area of the world we knew were doing the same thing. It seemed as natural as breathing.
>
> But much more exciting than breathing. Exhilarating. The sense of being in the right place at the right time, in step with a great movement in history, *part* of history, making history ourselves. We were part of a huge wave of women and we were going to remake everything. It gradually dawned on us that we didn't have to go out and join any movement. We were already in it. We were the Movement.[2]

If change was not immediate, then feminism at least enabled women to express their discontents, or, as Churchill argued in McFerran's interview, 'one of the things the Women's Movement has done is to show the way the traps work'.[3] The 'traps'

17

specific to theatre, which the women playwrights discussed in McFerran's interview, included male bias of their profession, the paucity of roles for women, the ways in which their voices had not been heard in the theatre, and the difficulties of combining a playwriting career with motherhood.

When questioned about her writing and feminism, Churchill observed:

> For years and years I thought of myself as a writer before I thought of myself as a woman, but recently I've found that I would say I was a feminist writer as opposed to other people saying I was. I've found that as I go out more into the world and get into situations which involve women what I feel is quite strongly a feminist position and that inevitably comes into what I write.[4]

Churchill went on to state that in her early writing she replicated the dominant tradition of the male writer by making her central characters with 'some knotty problem male', because as a 'woman writer' she felt she had to show that she too 'could do it'. Subsequently, however, 'realising the bad deal women have had' she made the 'characters with the knotty problems women'.[5] It was not just a question of concentrating on female rather than male characters, but of thinking through 'the "maleness" of the traditional structure of plays, with conflict and building in a certain way to a climax'.[6]

Among Churchill's work in the early 1970s, for example, are two unpublished plays which show her challenging the 'maleness' of writing and experimenting with an all-female and emergent feminist aesthetic: the radio play *Perfect Happiness* (1973) and the television play *Turkish Delight* (1974).[7] *Perfect Happiness* raises class and gender issues as two female office employees have an encounter with the middle-class wife of their employer. Set in a middle-class kitchen, it offers a critique of bourgeois domesticity enacted through women. The absent presence of the husband and employer figure, heard arriving at the end of the play after the working-class women have alleged they murdered him, is a technique also used in *Turkish Delight*, where the female characters are objectified and defined by their relationship to an unseen male figure, John. Set at a masquerade party where the women are in harem costuming, the aesthetic and ideological work of the play explores the kinds of issues which would preoccupy feminist film, and, subsequently, theatre studies in the 1980s: the gaze, objectification of women, the masquerade of femininity, and women as objects of exchange within a masculine, phallocentric economy'.[8] Whereas in the 1970s Churchill's feminist subjects and experimental forms both excited and baffled theatre critics (see for example the discussion of *Vinegar Tom*'s reception), in the 1980s, her critiques of gender – most especially those in *Cloud Nine* and *Top Girls* – helped to shape and to define the growing body of feminist writing, in theory, criticism and practice, which constitutes the field now recognized as feminist theatre studies.

In order to look at the emergent and evolving feminism of Churchill, the 'woman writer', I propose in this chapter to sample full-length stage plays from a ten-year period of playwriting: from the formative, gender-inflected critique of *Owners* (1972), to the mature, materialist-feminist inquiry of *Top Girls* (1982).

MASCULINE ECONOMY/FEMININE 'OTHER': *OWNERS*

Performed at the Royal Court Theatre Upstairs in 1972, Churchill's first full-length stage play is a critical analysis of Western capitalism's preoccupation with ownership. In staging her critique she brought together two working ideas: 'there was one idea going on about landlords and tenants, and then another about western aggressiveness and eastern passivity, and I realised that obviously the two could go together'.[9] Churchill dramatizes the 'haves and have nots' of the property market in her representation of the property-owning childless couple, Marion and Clegg, and the tenants, Alec and Lisa, who, in reduced circumstances, share rooms in a house with their two boys and Alec's mother. Lisa has a third child on the way as the play begins. 'Western aggressiveness and eastern passivity' are marked in the characters of Marion and Alec respectively. Churchill explains that gender role-reversal helped to make the contrast clear: 'the landlord became a woman, because that made the distinction better than if I'd had an active man and a passive woman'.[10]

As an ex-psychiatric patient who refused feminine condition-ing as part of her treatment, Marion, on exiting from hospital, elected to enter the financial world of property owning:

> CLEGG: When Marion was in hospital they tried to tell her she'd be happier and more sane as a good wife. Comb your hair and take an interest in your husband's work...But she wouldn't listen. She came out of there with staring eyes and three weeks later she bought her first house.
>
> (P1 10)

Like Marlene in *Top Girls*, Marion demonstrates that the capitalist impulse is not determined by the biological difference between male and female, but illustrates how women may also take on the values of the masculine. That Marion is driven by the desire to own and to control, but is not fully in control of her own actions, is signified in the directions for her costuming: '*her clothes are expensive but often badly matched, coming undone, slightly askew*' (P1 5).

The desire to own, to appropriate, is also shared by Marion's husband, Clegg. In the opening to the play Clegg is seen in his butcher's shop which is about to go out of business. However, Clegg explains that because he has no son to leave the business to there is no need for him to keep a business going:

> I envisaged a chain. Clegg and Son. I was still the son at the time. I would have liked a son myself once I was the Clegg. But now I've no business I don't need a son. Having no son I don't need a business'.
> (P1 9)

Clegg's rationale of his business and lack of a son and heir reflect the values, needs and ethos of capitalist and patriarchal systems.

By contrast, Alec and Lisa represent the dispossessed group: the tenants and victims of the owning classes. Passive resistance to Marion's active attempts to turn them out of their rented rooms is encoded in the figure of Alec. As Churchill observes, the dynamic between Alec and Marion is an embodiment of East and West values. Although Alec may be momentarily (sexually) engaged with Marion, he cannot be owned. He does not 'keep' (P1 32). Driven by her impulse to possess him, Marion declares her desire for Alec in terms of ownership, representing herself in imperialist and masculinist discourse:

I'm yours whether you want me or not. Have all the money and stay here too if that's what you want. Empires have been lost for love. Worlds well lost. We men of destiny get what we're after even if we're destroyed by it. And everyone else with us. We split the atom. Onward. Love me. (*P* 31)

Similarly, Clegg represents his relationship with Marion as a financial one; as a commodity for investment, profit and loss: 'I have invested heavily in Marion and don't intend to lose any part of my profit' (*P*1 56).

Alec, on the other hand, occupies a position which has no investment in a materialist economy. Having, as he explains to Marion, been troubled by the difficulty of not seeing the point of anything in life, including taking his own life (*P*1 47), Alec was able to transcend this position to a state of selfless passivity. When he takes the life of his mother by disconnecting her drip in hospital, the act is not an investment in an economy of the self, but a selfless act in the interests of the other. Similarly, when, in the conclusion of the play, he goes back into their burning home to save a baby, it is not his 'own' baby which he saves, but the baby from another family.

A central figure in Churchill's critique of ownership is Worsely, Marion's go-between who, acting on her behalf, tries to get tenants out of the properties Marion is buying. Clegg draws Worsely into his schemes to kill Marion – to possess her in the only way he can – and, at various times, Clegg and Marion enlist Worsely's help to fatally harm Alec – Clegg because he does not wish to lose Marion to Alec, and Marion because she cannot succeed in owning Alec. Much of the dark comedy in *Owners* is driven by Worsely's Ortonesque, farcical attempts to commit suicide. Worsely believes that he owns what he stands up in, his 'flesh and blood', in contrast to the Samaritan he describes as having befriended him, whom Worsely reports as arguing that God is 'the almighty landlord', and 'life is leasehold' (*P*1 35). Each time Worsely makes an appearance in the play, his body is marked by further self-inflicted damage, but he never quite succeeds in 'owning', that is, deciding the destiny of his own body.

Worsely is pivotal to Churchill's sinister style of comedy which arises out of the juxtaposition of light and dark tones. As drama scholar Martin Esslin, reviewing the production, described, 'what is remarkable is that this play which has such deep undertones is on the surface a highly amusing folk-comedy'.[11] Moreover as Esslin further observed, the juxtaposition of stylistic registers was also encoded in the original stage design for *Owners* which represented 'the hospital and the butcher's shop in their full naturalistic reality in front of a stylised back cloth'.[12]

Writing at the time of the production, Churchill identified Lisa as the 'victim of the story', and commented on how she had originally conceived the character in traditional terms as the woman who owns in a conventional way – 'my house, my husband, my children, my family'.[13] It is precisely her position as a woman within the traditional setting of home, husband, children and family, which makes her a victim. Reading *Owners* through Hélène Cixous's psychoanalytic framing of gender (as introduced in the discussion of *Schreber*), then Lisa is the Other which has to be colonized in the interests of the masculine 'selfsame'[14] (as is Alec when he refuses to be possessed by Marion). As the feminine Other, Lisa is the object of 'reappropriation'; she has to be owned, victimized, in order to confirm 'male privilege'; to repress the threat of castration.[15] This is clearly represented when in trying to get her baby back she allows Clegg to 'fuck' her. When Clegg reneges on his promise to help, she verbally assaults his masculinity: 'look at you sweating like a bit of hot fat, which is what you are. With your belly sagging like a black pudding and your poor little pork sausage' (*P1* 54). The meat imagery disavows rather than confirms the mastery of Clegg the butcher, or, read metaphorically, the butchery of the masculine, phallocentric order.

The victimization of Lisa is further, and perhaps most significantly, established in the loss of her baby to Marion and Clegg. Lisa's labour coincides with her discovery of the possibility of an affair between Marion and Alec being resumed. In her distress, and in labour, she refuses to bring the baby back to their home, saying she'd rather kill it, and then she challenges Marion to look after it. After the birth, and in a state of distress, she is coerced by Marion and Worsely into signing papers, and 'legally' makes over her baby to Marion and Clegg:

LISA: ...I can't read it.
MARION: No need.

WORSELY: Sign here.
LISA: After can I see the baby?
WORSELY: Don't drip all over the paper.
LISA: I want to see he's all right.
MARION: Of course he is.
LISA. Because later when I'm better I'll have him back.
WORSELY: He's very well taken care of. I wouldn't lie.
Lisa signs the paper.

(P1 42–3)

Churchill's dialogue heightens Lisa's disempowered position. She is no match for Worsely and Marion. She cannot even see the papers she is signing because of her tears. As psychologist and psychotherapist Phyllis Chesler, writing on surrogacy, adoption and custody issues, comments:

> What else is it but 'duress' to obtain a birth mother's signature by offering her hospital care or money when she's about to go into labor or has literally just given birth: when she's experiencing the most stressful moment of her life; when she has no legal advice, no job or housing or prospects…Most adoption papers are signed under 'duress' and most should therefore be considered illegal.[16]

What, in Lisa's case, begins as a form of protest – I'd rather kill or surrender my baby than accept the victim-position – rebounds under 'duress', as the birth mother signs away the rights to her baby. As actual surrogacy cases in the 1980s (the most (in)famous of these being the Baby M case in America)[17] have shown. 'owning' or buying babies is a class and gender issue: economic privilege empowers one class of mothers and fathers to buy: economic deprivation encourages disempowered mothers to sell. Lisa, as Churchill's dramatic representation of the economically deprived birth mother is, therefore, as much a victim of her class as of her gender.

As the birth father, Alec also critiques the politics of fatherhood which insist on the need for a son and heir. Alec does not seek to 'own' the baby as the natural father, and he cares for, indeed, as already noted, dies for a child which is not his 'own'. Unlike Clegg, who wants to keep the baby to fulfil his patriarchal desire for a son to inherit his business, or Marion, who wants the baby as her way of owning a part of Alec (P1 62), Alec does not assert his own claims to the child.

Legislative and social concern for the rights of the father has become a (frightening) issue for mothers in the 1990s.[18] Although this would inflect a revival of *Owners* differently to the play's 1970s social and cultural context, when motherhood figured on the middle-class feminist agenda as a contested site of maternal destiny,'[19] it would also invest the play with renewed topicality for the 1990s. Similarly, it is difficult to read another of Churchill's early radio plays, *Not Not Not Not Not Enough Oxygen*, broadcast in 1971, the year before *Owners*, where, in a world running out of natural resources, the birthing of children has to be sanctioned by a paid for licence, without thinking of the recently broadcast pictures of the dying rooms in China.[20] Churchill herself comments that 'it's slightly unnerving to read *Not...Oxygen* twenty years later. It's more obviously relevant now than it was then' (*S* intro).[21] Or, as poet and playwright Jackie Kay, interviewing Churchill in the late 1980s, put it to her, 'you seem to be able to predict popular concerns before they become popular'.[22]

Finally, it is also important to note in the context of the motherhood issue, that this was also one of immediate, personal concern to Churchill. She has described how her preliminary ideas for *Owners* were interrupted by a miscarriage, and how the writing of the play took place immediately, and rather hurriedly, in a few painful days, less than a week after coming out of hospital:

> I wrote it in three days. I'd just come out of hospital after a particularly gruesome late miscarriage. Still quite groggy and my arm ached because they'd given me an injection that didn't work. Into it went for the first time a lot of things that had been building up in me over a long time, political attitudes as well as personal ones.[23]

It is precisely this personal experience which increasingly politicized Churchill in moving from thinking of herself as a 'writer before I thought of myself as a woman', to thinking of herself as a 'feminist writer'.[24]

THE 'OFFSIDE BODY': *VINEGAR TOM*

Working within collaborative structures, with writers, companies, directors, and so on, also provided a way for the personal to become increasingly political and feminist in Churchill's career as a dramatist. For example, two of the other women playwrights involved in McFerran's 1977 interview, Mary O'Malley and Cherry Potter, worked with Churchill in the mid-1970s on a television piece, *Save It for the Minister*, which looked at sex discrimination. More significant, however, was her 1976 production of *Vinegar Tom* with Monstrous Regiment, and *Light Shining in Buckinghamshire*, written at the same time for Joint Stock (see chapter 3).

Up until this point, Churchill's writing career had been, as she described it, a 'solitary' one (P1 129) Chris Bowler of Monstrous Regiment recollected talking to Churchill about her more solitary career, as compared, for example, with life in the company:

> the difference ... is that she was involved in child care over a number of years and started writing for the radio at home. As a result she was always at one remove. I remember talking to her years ago when she said that that was what it felt like, being at one remove. She felt that being at home she had missed out on things that we were involved in.[25]

In consequence, Churchill was both excited and daunted by the prospect of being able to work on a feminist piece with and for a feminist company: 'I felt briefly shy and daunted, wondering if I would be acceptable, then happy and stimulated by the discovery of shared ideas and the enormous energy and feeling of possibilities in the still new company' (P1 129).

It was the Liberation Movement which brought Churchill into contact with the women from Monstrous Regiment (they met on an abortion march). As Churchill has commented elsewhere, 'you tend to think of your own development only having to do with yourself and it's exciting to discover it in a historical context', also noting that the higher profiling of work by women playwrights (as discussed in the McFerran interview), was linked to the growth in the 1970s of new writing, fringe theatre and feminist companies.[26] Monstrous Regiment was founded in the mid-1970s by Chris Bowler, Gillian Hanna and Mary McCusker as a response to the male bias of the theatre and an urgent need to find a 'space' in which to explore their socialist-feminist ideas and politics in theatrical practice. *Vinegar Tom* was their second production, after their inaugural tour of *Scum*, which was co-scripted by Claire Luckham and Chris Bond and set in the Paris Commune of 1871.

Vinegar Tom is set in seventeenth-century rural England, and is organized into twenty-one scenes whose dramatic action is punctuated by contemporary songs to be performed '*in modern dress*' and not as '*part of the action*' (P1 133). Looking back at the critical record of *Vinegar Tom*'s reception, it is the structural movement between the seventeenth-century setting and the contemporary songs which was received as problematic in terms of dramatic form. David Zane Mairowitz's commentary on *Vinegar Tom* sets Churchill's 'new feminist dimensions' against the 'pinnacle' of plays on witchcraft, Arthur Miller's *The Crucible*.[27] Churchill's socialist-feminist critique of a persecuted community of women is judged against the classic realist form which places the tragic hero (male) as the persecuted centre of dramatic action and attention. Because Churchill does not choose to draw us into a harrowing, tragic study of a persecuted (male) individual, but, reflecting the political ethos of Monstrous Regiment's style of ensemble organization and playing, looks to a collective representation of woman-centred oppression, the scenes are dismissed as 'only sketched': the desire for 'dramatic elaboration' is seen as thwarted by the 'song interruptions'. 'The playtext', Mairowitz elaborates, 'is not strong enough to withstand the breaking of its rhythm and antagonism of the musical interludes'.[28]

Similarly, despite a positive review which concluded by declaring *Vinegar Tom* an 'impressive feminist play, and an impressive feminist theatre production', feminist critic Michelene Wandor 'spent some time on the few jarring [song] moments' partly 'because the integration of different art forms in one production are [sic] difficult and perhaps need more analysis than a straightforward either/or play/musical'.[29] However, other commentators were able to take Wandor's 'either/or' query further, and to grasp that Churchill's experimentation with form did not represent a failed attempt to write in a canonical (male) tradition but was a way of exploring the possibilities of a feminist aesthetic. Commenting on the production of *Vinegar Tom*, Ned Chaillet claimed that the company had 'found a style which demands our serious attention'.[30] Gillian Hanna explained how this 'style' was a response to breaking down conventions of dramatic form, stating that 'we knew that we had to have the music to smash that regular and acceptable theatrical form', in the interests of exploring what she identified as a 'counter-cultural', feminist style of performance.[31]

The challenge to form, the 'unfixing' of boundaries, are now widely recognized strategies of feminist theatre which explore the liminal in the interests of challenging the sign of Woman. Read from this perspective, the songs are a critical and crucial key to the formal and ideological work of the play. As they are to be performed out of character and in modern dress, they create the opportunity for the performer to insert her body into the performance text as a si[gh]te of disruption. This is more than an oversimplistic linking of past and present, as Wandor argued,[32] but offers a way of representing the marginal and the absent in dominant systems of representation.

The first two songs, for example, 'Nobody Sings' and 'Oh Doctor', are specifically concerned with the invisibility of women represented by the sign of Woman. 'Nobody Sings' references the menstruating body and the cycle of the ageing body whose 'cunt' becomes 'sore and dry' in old age (Pl 142). Women are 'nobody' when they are young and attractive (because objectified by the gaze), and 'nobody' when they are old because ageing renders them invisible, nonrepresentable. However, the song and performer, distanced from the dramatic action, combine to create a critical space in which to see beyond the limits of representation. As French feminist Catherine Clément, writing alongside of Hélène Cixous, argues, the menstruating body signifies both 'order and disorder'; 'it is precisely in this natural periodicity that fear, terror, that which is offside in the symbolic system will lodge itself'.[33] Making the absent body of menstruating and ageing women present is a way of showing the threat which women pose to the symbolic (i.e. the dominant order); a way of 'showing the cracks in an overall system'.[34] Significant in this respect is the juxtaposition of 'Nobody Sings' with Scene Four and the Gestus of the farmer's wife Margery churning the butter which 'won't come' (Pl 142). The phallocentric order is disturbed by the 'unnatural' presence of the 'offside' body.

The lyrics of 'Oh Doctor' are voiced by a woman, positioned as the disempowered patient, who pleads to know what is wrong with her; asks to have her body put back together again and to be allowed a sense of herself. The song functions as a critique of mechanistic male medicine in which women are denied ownership of their bodies and cannot be represented as a whole, merely as holes which the doctor examines with his 'metal eye' (P1 150). The 'metal eye' is evocative of psychoanalyst Luce Irigaray's speculum, which the gynaecologist uses to enter and to 'see' inside a woman's womb, but which is also the specular gaze of phallocentric desire, in which woman is represented as marginalized Other.[35] The song is inserted into Scene Six which depicts Betty, a middle-class young woman, diagnosed as 'hysteric', tied to a chair, and about to be bled as a means of controlling her body which is in revolt against her present (patriarchal) home and her future (patriarchal) prison, marriage. Framed around the *Gestus* of Betty's bleeding body (the act of showing Betty's relation to structures of social control), the song allows women to speak outside or beyond the male system of control in which the female body is fragmented, violated, abused and silenced.

These songs which image the subversive female body are echoed in the seventeenth-century community of women portrayed in the dramatic scenes. Alice, a young, unmarried mother, represents the sexually active body and woman as castrating figure. Scene Thirteen, for example, shows Alice 'giving' Jack, a married farmer who lusts after and blames Alice for his impotence, his penis back:

JACK: Give it me then. Come on.
SUSAN: Wait, she can't move, leave her alone.
JACK: Give it me.
Alice puts her hand between his thighs.
ALICE: There. It's back.
JACK: It is. It is back. Thank you, Alice, I wasn't sure you were a witch till then.

(P1 64)

The birthing body is represented in Alice's friend Susan, who is married and is constantly either pregnant or miscarrying. The ageing body is figured through Alice's mother Joan, and the body of the hysteric is represented in the figure of Betty, the middle-class woman who runs away from marriage.

Not all of the songs take the body as their focus, 'Something to Burn' (P1 154) thematizes the marginalization of oppressed groups – not just women, but also 'lunatics', 'blacks' and 'Jews'. 'If You Float' (P1 170) highlights women's situation as a 'catch-22': float and you are a witch; sink and you die anyway. The song critiques patriarchal 'logic' which manipulates sign-systems, arbitrarily inventing and re-inventing the 'signs' of Woman's 'evil' doing. In the 'logic' of this sign-system a woman who uses her knowledge and skills to help other women, like Ellen who is skilled in midwifery and practises abortion, can be (mis)-represented and condemned as a witch.

'Lament for the Witches' (P1 175) asks us to think about who are the witches now, and to what extent we may also be persecuted and scapegoated, and 'Evil Women' (P1 178–9), following the last scene, in which, in the manner of a music-hall routine, Kramer and Sprenger deliver lines from the *Malleus Maleficarum, The Hammer of Witches*, critiques the projection of evil on to women by the sexually inadequate man. This echoes Jack blaming Alice for his sexual impotence, but reiterates the point in a modern context. This is the contemporary man who sees 'evil women' on the 'movie screen' or in his 'own wet dream' (P1 178). Gillian Hanna explains that some spectators were critical of the play, or more specifically the songs, for constantly making parallels between the past and present, but she argues that the performers felt it was politically necessary:

> We had a very real feeling that we didn't want to allow the audience to get off the hook by regarding it [*Vinegar Tom*] as a period piece, a piece of very interesting history. Now a lot of people felt their intelligence was affronted by that. They said: 'I don't know why these people have to punctuate what they are saying by these modern songs. We're perfectly able to draw conclusions about the world today from historical parallels.' Actually, I don't believe that and, in any case, we can't run that risk. For every single intelligent man who can draw the parallels, there are dozens who don't. It's not that they can't. It's that they won't.[36]

In the seventeenth-century scenes, those women who are most marginalized in the community, because of their 'outsider' status and their lack of material status within the patriarchal and capitalist economy, are the most persecuted, and the most at risk. Alice, for example, is representative of the economically deprived single-mother group. She is separated from her child while witch-finder Packer tries to make her confess to being a witch:

> PACKER: Why won't you confess and make this shorter?...
> ALICE:...I want my boy.
> PACKER: Then you should have stayed at home at night with him and not gone out after the devil.
> ALICE: I want him.
> PACKER: How could a woman be a filthy witch and put her child in danger?
> ALICE: I didn't.
> PACKER: Night after night, it's well known.
> ALICE: But what's going to happen to him? He's only got me.
> PACKER: He should have a father...
>
> (P1 171)

Packer's cross-examination of Alice bears a frightening resemblance to the 1990s crusade against 'lone mothers' and 'home alone' children by right-wing politicians who, for example, have argued that it is '"good Christian doctrine" to stop single women having children before they...formed stable relationships', or have 'defended the Government's right to speak out against the impact of single parenthood on crime and social breakdown.'[37] Another example, perhaps, of Churchill 'anticipat[ing] crucial issues'?

Those women in *Vinegar Tom* who are either materially better off, like Betty, and/or whose status is sanctioned by marriage, like Margery and Susan, are also victims of a male-dominated society, and are particularly oppressed by the social construct of the family, as highlighted in the song 'If Everybody Worked as Hard as Me' (P1 159–60). The *Gestus* of Scene Nineteen, Margery offers her prayer of thanks to God, the Father, while Joan and Ellen are hanged, effectively critiques the prisonhouse of religion ('you have shown your power in destroying the wicked'), patriarchy ('Bless Miss Betty's marriage and let her live happy') and capitalism ('Bless Jack...and give us the land') (P1 174).

Writing the songs for *Vinegar Tom* was a new experience for Churchill, but the ethos of feminist collectives encouraged and supported that acquisition of new skills. Churchill went on to write more songs for another Monstrous Regiment production: *Floorshow* (1977). *Floorshow* was scripted between Churchill, Bryony Lavery, Michelene Wandor and David Bradford, and used the cabaret form to tackle women's rights issues such as sexism and sexual division of labour. It was a question of raising feminist issues and politicizing theatrical form:

> We saw women acting as comperes and cracking bitterly funny jokes, and men talking about their own sexism: women refusing to act the ventriloquist's dummy, and men singing about stereotypical nursery rhymes and minding the baby.[38]

Looking back at *Owners* and forward to *Vinegar Tom*, it is possible to see how important the experience of working with the feminist company Monstrous Regiment was to the emergent 'woman writer'. Moreover, we begin to see how feminist concerns were moving to a more central position in Churchill's work during the 1970s as evidenced in her 1979 staging of sexual politics: *Cloud Nine*.

PERFORMING GENDER: *CLOUD NINE*

In between beginning and finishing *Vinegar Tom* for Monstrous Regiment, Churchill began her first workshop with director Max Stafford-Clark and the Joint Stock company with whom she was to establish an important and enduring working relationship. *Light Shining in Buckinghamshire*, detailed in the following chapter, was their first collaborative venture. *Cloud Nine*, Churchill's second production for Joint Stock, came about because Churchill and Max Stafford-Clark wanted to do another show together. As Churchill explained in an interview, she did not at first conceive of sexual politics, the topic she really wanted to work on, as a Joint Stock project:

> Joint Stock at that point was such a male company...It seemed the last company which you would think of doing a show like that, and of course as soon as I had said that, we realized that was a very good reason for in fact doing it.[39]

The 'offside' body which disrupts the symbolic in *Vinegar Tom* is a key focus in the sexual politics of *Cloud Nine* which takes the body as a critical si[gh]te of gender representation. It is written in two acts: the first uses a colonial setting to critique the Victorian values of Empire and family; the second traces the characters from Act One to a London setting in 1979, although the time shift for the characters is only twenty-five years. The continuity of linear history is, therefore, displaced by a historical memory of sexual politics; the past is physically marked in and on the body of the performer, present.

Cross-gender and cross-racial casting, and the doubling of roles are techniques central to Churchill's destabilizing of fixed sexual identities determined by dominant heterosexual ideology. The theatrical device of cross-dressing in *Cloud Nine* has been of particular interest to feminist theatre scholarship. As Sue-Ellen Case and Jeanie K. Forte, looking to examples of a 'new feminist theater practice' located in the 'critique of the self', explain, *Cloud Nine* uses the colonial setting and cross-gender casting to show a 'world of alternative identities and practices while demonstrating the link between dominant ideology and institutionalized gender roles and sexuality'.[40] The ideological pleasure of cross-dressing in *Cloud Nine* is that it allows the spectator the possibility of seeing beyond 'institutionalized gender roles and sexuality' by crossing vestimentary signs of masculinity and femininity with the 'wrong' body. This is demonstrated in the opening sequence as the patriarch, Clive, introduces his family gathered around the flagpole displaying the Union Jack: Betty his wife, 'man's creation', is played by a man; Edward his son is played by a woman; his Black man servant, Joshua, is played by a white actor, and Victoria, his daughter, represented by a doll, is, like her governess and Clive's mother-in-law, not important enough to be properly introduced (*P1* 251–2). Although the characters, oppressed by the imperialist roles assigned to them by Clive, affirm their identities linguistically, consenting to their given roles as what they 'want to be', visually their 'offside' bodies disrupt the construction of sexual and, in the case of Joshua, racial identities.

The tension between the 'fixing' and 'unfixing' of gender construction structures the comic play of Act One, and climaxes in the farcical 'heterosexual' marriage ceremony (a ritual conventionally used in dramatic comedy to mark the restoration of family values), between the explorer Harry, who is gay, and the governess, Ellen, who is a lesbian. Both Harry and Ellen are 'offside' bodies in the symbolic which have to be 'corrected'. Homosexuality is viewed as 'a disease more contagious than diphtheria' (P1 283), and Clive advocates marriage for Harry as a 'cure' – just as Dr Hodge 'cures' his patients and friends through aversion therapy in *Lovesick*. Harry, therefore, is to be 'cleansed' of his homosexuality and to be made safe to society through marriage.

As a lesbian, Ellen is not visible. Although Clive listens to Joshua's gossip about the possibility of an affair between Harry and Betty, he will not acknowledge the possibility of Ellen making love to his wife (P1 285). When Ellen kisses and declares her love to Betty, what the spectator sees is a man (Betty) kissing a woman (Ellen) (P1 271). Churchill's cross-gendering device highlights the visibility of heterosexuality, marking the invisibility of lesbian identity and desire.

Similarly, although Mrs Saunders, a neighbouring widow who seeks protection from Clive when the 'natives' are restless, is a heterosexual woman, as a woman on her own she poses a threat to the family unit and, like Ellen, must also be expelled. (Interestingly, in the original Joint Stock production these two roles were played by the same actress.) The Victorian double standard of sexual morality is critiqued as Clive, who continually lusts after Mrs Saunders, is imaged under her skirt having sex with her at the Christmas picnic, as voices off-stage encode the values of family and Empire in the singing of a Christmas carol (P1 263–4). Mrs Saunders dislikes Clive but, in keeping with her spirit of independence, does enjoy sex. However, there is no sexual gratification for her in an act which centres purely on Clive's climax and ejaculation. While Clive hurriedly 'comes' and rushes ('all sticky') to rejoin his family, Mrs Saunders is left asking 'What about me?' (P1 264). In her recent theorizing of a 'corporeal feminism', Elizabeth Grosz has analysed the 'come' or 'ejaculation shot' in pornography not as an imaging of male pleasure, but as a masculine fantasy of female pleasure:

> Pornography, at least in part, offers itself to the (male) spectator as a form of knowledge and conceptual/perceptual mastery of the enigmas of female sexuality but is in fact his own projection of sexual pleasure. The come shot is thus no longer an unmediated representation and demonstration of his pleasure (as one would

expect): it becomes an index of his prowess to generate her pleasure. His sexual specificity is not the object of the gaze but remains a mirror or rather a displacement of her pleasure (or at least his fantasy of her pleasure).[41]

Churchill's 'ejaculation shot', or tableau, creates a *Gestus* which indexes the wider social context in which female pleasure is displaced by the male fantasy of female sexuality and desire. This is underlined in verbal play, as Clive mistakes Mrs Saunders's unsatisfied pleasure for a 'voracious' sexual appetite, and through the visual comedy of Clive climaxing underneath the skirt of a disappointed Mrs Saunders. The Victorian skirt functions as a sign of the socially constructed feminine (especially foregrounded in the case of the 'man-made' Betty), which displaces female desire and keeps the female body (and pleasures of the body) hidden from view.

That the 'desired' purification of Harry and Ellen in Act One will not be achieved, is signalled in the closing moments of their wedding ceremony at the end of the act, when the artifice of the occasion is exposed, or literally blown away, as Joshua shoots Clive. The shooting of Clive by his Black servant is a further indication of how the violent colonization of Black skins forced into white, 'pure' masks, in turn leads to acts of violence (as dramatized in *The Hospital*.) But it especially underlines the dangers of enforcing heterosexual identity and desire. As feminist drama scholar Susan Carlson explains:

> In this parody of the typical comic happy ending, Churchill reiterates her act-long critique of social and comic tradition. Clive's celebration of the marriage – the speech with which the act ends – is, after the exposures of the act, no longer just farcical but dangerous...
>
> In exposing the empire in this Wildean fashion, she also makes tangible the danger of our consenting to the traditional stereotypes and patterns of comedy. On our road to the predictable comic ending, where are we left, when types exist only in perverted forms and when emotions find expression only clandestinely?[42]

As in *Lovesick*, the pleasure for the spectator – or, in the case of the radio play, the listener – lies in the explosion of heterosexual strait-jacketing; the *jouissance* of the marginal or 'unnatural' body disturbing, disrupting, and destroying the sexual 'norm'.

Like the characters in the play, the performers involved in

workshopping *Cloud Nine* also had to confront their own sexual prejudices and ways in which they had encountered or been oppressed by sexual stereotyping, and so on. Actor Antony Sher explains:

> Throughout the workshop we each took turns to tell our own life stories and to answer questions on our sexual experiences and lifestyles. It was nervewracking to contemplate (and far more revealing than stripping naked would have been) and so it is to the credit of the group that these sessions became the most exhilarating of all. Through them the real meaning of sexual politics was becoming clear. Each of us was secure in our separate territory male, female, gay, straight, married, single, or whatever; brainwashed by different upbringings and prejudices. However liberal we each previously thought ourselves, we were now face to face with 'the others' and so many preconceptions were proving to be wrong.[43]

Churchill has also explained how the Victorian setting for Act One reflected the way in which the actors felt that they had been brought up with Victorian attitudes which they had to rebel against in their own lives:

> When we discussed our backgrounds it occurred to us it was as if everyone felt they had been born almost in the Victorian age. Everyone had grown up with quite conventional and old-fashioned expectations about sex and marriage and felt that they themselves had had to make enormous break-aways and leaps to change their lives from that. That was why it was an appropriate image for that to set the people's childhoods in Victorian times.[44]

Although the 1970s setting for Act Two implies a more liberal time period than the Victorian past, characters are still seen to be struggling with gender roles and identities: they still have a number of prejudices and preconceptions to explore. The violence of the colonial setting (actual and metaphorical) is alluded to again through reference to the struggles in Northern Ireland (see *P1* 291, 303, 310–11). Churchill explained how they 'looked at England's relation to Ireland and how it is like a male/female relationship'. 'The traditional view of the Irish' she continued 'is that they're charming, irresponsible, close to nature, all the things that people tend to think about women'.[45]

If Clive failed to give Mrs Saunders pleasure, then Martin, the 'new man' married to Victoria (the doll in Act One), under the guise of being liberated and wanting to discuss his wife's sexual pleasure, is, in reality, merely obsessed with his own sexual performance: 'My one aim is to give you pleasure. My one aim is to give you rolling orgasms like I do other women. So why the hell don't you have them?' (P1 300–301). Just as Mrs Saunders struggled to find ways of managing her life independently, Victoria too is trying to work out her sexuality and to consider a career move which means working away from her child, sexual partners and immediate family.

The actress who played Ellen and Mrs Saunders in Act One now takes on the role of Lin, a single lesbian mother, in love with Victoria. From being a lesbian who looked after someone else's children, Ellen, as Lin, now has a child of her own, and the possibility of a lesbian relationship, rather than the 'safety' of heterosexual marriage. Where Ellen as a lesbian was invisible, Lin speaks her desire for women and for Victoria in particular, in a way which makes her lesbian identity visible. Edward, on the other hand, is concerned that his gay identity be kept a secret in order not to lose his job as a gardener (P1 292). As his gay relationship with Gerry breaks down, he rejects a partnered gay identity for a lesbian-identified position, choosing not to live in a couple, but to live with his sister Lin and the two children.

As in Act One, the fixing and unfixing of sexual identities, as, for example, illustrated in Edward's case, also provides a structuring device for Act Two. Thematically, it is also fore-grounded in an incantation scene in which Victoria, Lin and Edward pray to a female goddess and ask her to give them back 'the history we haven't had', to 'make us the women we can't be' (P1 308). The call to the goddess of 'breasts', 'cunts', 'fat bellies and babies', 'and blood blood blood' (P1 309), invokes the absent 'offside' female body, which they need to remake desire and identity beyond the conventional ordering of sexuality.

Moving beyond the gaze of the patriarch who is now reduced to a child, as the actor who played Clive in Act One doubles as Lin's child Cathy in Act Two, is figured in the representation of Betty. Betty announces that she is leaving Clive and making a life for herself. As she renegotiates relationships with her family as part of the leaving process, she also explores her sexuality. Having been driven away from auto-eroticism by her mother when she was a child, she narrates the rediscovery of her body and her ability to give herself sexual pleasure. Within the objectified gaze of her husband her own desire was absent: 'I thought if Clive wasn't looking at me there wasn't a person there' (P1 316). Touching herself, she was fearful that her 'hand might go through space' (P1 316), but she finds her own body, her own pleasures, her own orgasm, unmediated by a male presence. Hugh Rorrison, reviewing for *Plays and Players*, argued that Julie Covington's performance as Betty 'as she probes to find the personality which Victorian marriage denied her is the strongest plea for liberal attitudes in the play'.[46] In the closing image of *Cloud Nine* Clive, stuck in the patriarchal past from Act One, enters to condemn the 'new' Betty, but his presence is displaced as he exits and Betty embraces her self from Act One. The final image of the split self uniting offers women the possibility of a subjectivity beyond the objectification of the gaze.

Churchill's dramatization of sexual politics in *Cloud Nine* foregrounds the ways in which gay identities are marginalized by heterosexuality, but does not lose sight of the ways in which women are oppressed by dominant doll-like (as suggested by Victoria) representations of femininity and the absence of female desire. Part of the play's attraction and an aspect of its uniqueness is that it manages to cover a broad spectrum of sexual politics, rather than focusing on one sexually oppressed group:

> One of the things I wanted very much to do, in *Cloud 9* ... was to write a play about sexual politics that would *not* just be a woman's thing. I felt there were quite a few women's groups doing plays from that point of view. And gay groups ... There was nothing that also involved straight men. Max [Stafford Clark], the director, even said, at the beginning 'Well shouldn't you perhaps be doing this with a woman director?' He didn't see that it was his subject as well.[47]

From the sexual politics in *Cloud Nine* as a 'subject' which concerns us all, Churchill turned her attention in *Top Girls* to the subject of feminism as an issue of immediate, although not exclusive, concern to women.

'US AND THEM': *TOP GIRLS*

Although *Top Girls* was staged in 1982, ten years after *Owners*, ideas for the play began in the late 1970s. Churchill recalls that as early as 1977–8 she was making notes on Dull Gret, a character from the opening dinner scene, and had also had an idea about staging a play in which a lot of women from the past have coffee with a woman in the present.[48] She was also becoming increasingly concerned about the dangers of bourgeois feminism:

> It was also that Thatcher had just become prime minister; and also I had been to America for a student production of *Vinegar Tom* and had been talking to women there who were saying things were going very well: they were getting far more women executives, women vice-presidents and so on. And that was such a different attitude from anything I'd ever met here, where feminism tends to be much more connected with socialism and not so much to do with women succeeding on the sort of capitalist ladder. All of those ideas fed into *Top Girls*.[49]

While *Vinegar Tom* caught the wave of excitement generated by the Women's Movement, *Top Girls* coincided with the moment when women needed to look more closely at the complexities of feminism; to question the 1970s politics of bonding, of sisterhood, through a politics of difference.

Top Girls opens with a celebration dinner at a restaurant for 'top girl' Marlene who has just been promoted to managing director of the employment agency she works for. Celebrating her success are the women travellers, Isabella Bird and former courtesan Lady Nijo, Dull Gret and Patient Griselda taken from a Brueghel painting and a Chaucerian tale respectively, and Joan, the female 'heresy' believed to have been pope. This assembly of women, therefore, defies the logic of historical, chronological, and spatial representation, as Churchill plays with the dramatic conventions which traditionally govern time, place and character.

After the dinner the action moves to a series of short scenes in the employment agency in which a number of women seeking jobs and promotion are interviewed by Marlene and her 'top girl' agency colleagues. Cutting across these scenes is the narrative of Angie, purportedly Marlene's niece, but who is actually Marlene's real daughter. A final act, which introduces a further time shift as it is set a year earlier than the Agency scenes, stages a hard-hitting 'us and them', class-gender-confrontation scene between Marlene and her working-class sister Joyce, who has raised Angie as her own daughter.

Top Girls explores both inter- and intra-sexual oppression. The narrative threads of the dinner party conversation are signifi-cantly marked by a discourse of intersexual oppression as the women share their experiences of being daughters, wives, mistresses and mothers. Their dialogue records both patriarchal oppression and the desire to move beyond the conventional gender divide. Just as in *Cloud Nine* the characters refuse the 'fixing' of gender roles, linguistically the women in *Top Girls* mark their rejection of being represented as the feminine 'other': Isabella gave up the confines of domestic life for travel, Nijo turned from courtesan to nun, and Joan violated the 'natural' (patriarchal) order by becoming pope. The drunken climax of the dinner scene verbally and physically enacts a violent rejection of intersexual oppression as, in parallel 'texts', Gret calls on her women neighbours to leave their 'baking or washing' to fight the 'devils' in hell, to go 'where the evil come from and pay the bastards out' (*P2* 82); Nijo recalls conspiring with other women to beat the Emperor; Joan spews out chunks of Latin and is sick in the corner, and even Patient Griselda protests that she had rather Walter had not put her to the test as he did. However, it is significant that these 'texts' are parallel rather than interactive. Despite Marlene's plea to Joan to shut up, and Isabella's command that everyone listen to Gret because she has been to hell (*P2* 82), the women are largely and self-centredly caught up in their own individual narratives. The inability to listen to and to share experiences with women, is indicative of intrasexual oppression, and underscored in this first act through Churchill's use of overlapping dialogue – a technique she had recently experimented with in her short play *Three More Sleepless Nights*.[50]

Further, as a counterpoint to the desire to exit from the scene of oppression, the feminine is verbally and visually signed on and through the body. Nijo, the courtesan, for example, describes her love of clothes, silks designed to attract and to please the Emperor, and Griselda's from-peasant-girl-toprincess narrative signifies the objectification of the feminine in the heterosexual, male gaze. Moreover, as Elin Diamond has observed, the actual costuming of each of these 'top girl' women in the dinner scene 'points to the elaborate historical text that covers her body', marking the 'cost' of 'hav[ing] entered Western representation'.[51] Rejection of the masculine is, therefore, constantly warring with the physical and verbal registers of patriarchal oppression. This is further indexed in the constant juxtaposition of emotional opposites, such as laughter and misery (the women laugh at Joan, the pregnant Pope, but are moved to silence as she announces she was stoned to death at the birth of her baby, *P2* 71), and the 'unfixing' of the significant and the insignificant (Isabella recalls the death of her father and in the same breath places an order from the menu, *P2* 58).

The 'cost' of 'Western representation' is clearly encoded in the figure of Marlene, the one main character from the present (there is also the waitress), a woman who, like Marion in *Owners* is constructed as the 'conventional man'. Her identification with dominant, masculine values is reflected in the way in which actress and role are constant, unlike the 'unfixing' strategies encoded in the doubling of other characters. The figure of Marlene demonstrates how the acceptance and 'success' of a woman in the workplace requires very careful self-presentation. Like Isabella who 'always travelled as a lady', Marlene takes care not to wear trousers in the office (*P2* 62). The projection of a 1980s 'Superwoman' image as dramatized in the office scenes, demonstrates a need for adept role playing between high-powered lady and ball-breaking boss. Power-dressing role play does not, however, include representation of the maternal. Children and a career in a man's world are mutually exclusive, as is powerfully illustrated in Pope Joan's narrative of being stoned to death for birthing a baby, and Marlene's relationship, or rather absence of a relationship, with her daughter.

Critics have sometimes questioned the ideological purpose of Marlene, or *Top Girls* in general, asking whether to read Marlene and the play as a celebration of women's achievements or a critique of bourgeois feminism? A rather confused John Russell Taylor, for example, asked of Marlene 'well is she a heroine or isn't she?', and summed up the play as one 'which sends you out asking questions and trying to work out, not disagreeably, just what it is you have been watching'.[52] However, Marlene's male-identified subject positioning is an unequivocal indexing of Churchill's critique of bourgeois feminism. While the doubling and overlapping techniques suggest fragmentation and the possibility of 'unfixing', Marlene's stable positioning functions as an oppressive 'block' to the desires and aspirations of other women. This is especially true of her positioning in relation to Angie's narrative.

Structurally, *Top Girls* has either been presented as two acts, as in the original production, played with one interval, or as a three-act drama, played with two intervals. Churchill states her own preference for the three-act version which she claims makes the 'structure clearer: Act One, the dinner; Act Two, Angie's story; Act Three, the year before' (P2 54). As Churchill clarifies, the three-act structure underlines Angie's 'story' as the focus of the second act. This refuses an interpretation of the office scenes as a celebration of Marlene, the achiever in the workplace, by positioning the underachiever, Angie, shown in her back yard at home and as a visitor to the office, as the focus of the act and the key site of intrasexual oppression. This is visually represented in Angie wearing a dress bought for her by Marlene which is now too small for her (P2 98). The dress signifies the 'misfit' or gap between Angie's desire to be like the (well-dressed), career woman Marlene, and Marlene's dismissal of her own daughter's career aspirations as a 'packer in Tesco more like' (P2 120).

Unlike the voices of the middle-class women which dominate the linguistic space, 'dull' Angie, like Gret in Act One, is relatively silent. (Significantly, in the original Royal Court production the roles of Angie and Gret were doubled by one actress.) In Act Two Scene Two, Angie struggles to hold her own in the verbal power-play of teenage rivalry between herself and her younger, but brighter, friend Kit:

ANGIE: You know the kitten?
KIT: Which one?
ANGIE: There only is one. The dead one.
KIT: What about it?
ANGIE: I heard it last night.
KIT: Where?

41

ANGIE: Out here. In the dark. What if I left you here in the dark all
    night?
KIT: You couldn't. I'd go home.
ANGIE: You couldn't.
KIT: I'd / go home.
ANGIE: No you couldn't, not if I said.
KIT: I could.

(P2 89)

However, linguistically, Angie repeatedly fails to assert authority over Kit. Like the disempowered interviewees at the agency,
she is no match for her brighter friend who sees a future for
herself as a nuclear physicist. Angie's silenced, sleeping
presence in the office scene at the close of the act, as Marlene
verbalizes her destiny in the line, 'she's not going to make it (P2
120), prefigures her waking-nightmare state at the close of the
play as, in Marlene's presence, she delivers the final, one-word
line, 'Frightening' (P2 141).

Churchill's socialist-feminist critique of bourgeois-feminist
values is highlighted in the final act which stages the class
confrontation between the two sisters. Joyce, as the working-
class mother-figure who has taken care of Angie, is represented
as economically, socially and culturally 'deprived', relative to
Marlene's 'top girl' success. But the devalued mothering of a
child which is not her own (rather like Alec in Owners who saves
a baby who 'belongs' to someone else) calls into question the
value placed on Marlene's 'childless' career. As Sue-Ellen Case
summarizes: 'the economic situation has created two choices for
women: the relative economic poverty of child-rearing, or the
emotional alienation of success within the structures of
capitalism'.[53]

Churchill's representation of Marlene and Joyce is echoed in
Isabella's narrative of her sister Hennie. As the first guest to
arrive at Marlene's dinner party, Isabella's opening conversation
centres on Hennie and she is quick to ask Marlene whether she,
too, has a sister (P2 55). Like Marlene and Joyce, Isabella and
Hennie were separated by geography. Isabella would leave for
months at a time on her exotic foreign travels, returning to
Hennie who stayed put in Tobermory, Scotland.[54] However,
where Isabella was devoted to her sister and sustained
communication through letter writing about her travels (P2

42

65), Marlene's obsession with her career means she hardly sees her sister, or her daughter. In Act Three it is established that Marlene has not visited Joyce and Angie for six years (P2 135). Unlike Hennie, all that Joyce and Angie receive while Marlene is away in America is the clichéd wish-you-were-here postcard which Angie treasures (P2 129).

The travel discourse of Isabella (and Nijo) illustrates how geographic mobility relates to independence. Similarly, while Marlene has enjoyed working in America and now has the excitement of running the agency in London, Joyce remains trapped in their home town (the 'back yard' setting of Act Two Scene Two suggests a working-class, terraced, urban setting), with few employment opportunities for women. Women seeking jobs through the employment agency also equate travel with career opportunities: Jeanine would like to travel (P2 86), and Shona fantasizes about an expensive car and high-powered selling up and down the M1 (P2 117). Angie's trip to London to see her 'aunt' is also her travel adventure which expresses a desire for change. However, Joyce, Angie, and the young women seeking jobs are blocked both intrasexually by the middle-class career women, and intersexually, by educational, familial and economic factors which keep them geographically and socially bound to their milieu and class, a point which Churchill would develop centrally in her next play, *Fen* (see chapter 4).

Although some spectators and critics, like John Russell Taylor, may have been confused by the formal and ideological purpose of Marlene and *Top Girls*, for others, and for women especially, it provided intense pleasures. *Top Girls* specifically, and Churchill's woman-centred, feminist theatre generally, pleasures the (feminist) spectator through the dynamics of dramatic composition and political content. As Joseph Marohl argues in an introduction to Churchill's theatre and an analysis of *Top Girls*, 'what the audience experiences during the performance, then, is defamiliarization of the ordinary (alienation effect) and the subversion of positive ideologues about gender, social hierarchies, and chronology'.[55] In contrast to some first-wave feminist drama which concentrated on the political at the expense of the theatrical, Churchill pleasured her (feminist) spectator through theatrical style and her representation of gender issues. As Gillian Hanna's comments on *Vinegar Tom* illustrated, experimenting with form is a way of representing women's (absent) experiences; of exploring the possibilities of a 'counter-cultural' aesthetics. This was exciting for women performers, spectators and, subsequently, feminist theatre scholars who, in the 1980s, became increasingly interested in the theorization of a possible feminist performance style and aesthetics.

Top Girls affords a further pleasure for the female spectator in so far as it represents an all-female community, played by an all-female cast. Creating a women-only stage picture was not uncommon in alternative feminist theatre-making in the 1970s and early 1980s. For example, the Women's Theatre Group which, like Monstrous Regiment, was established in the mid-1970s, made it a company policy to perform plays with only roles for women. In a mainstream context, however, women-only plays tended to succeed on mainstream terms, which is not surprising given, as McFerran's interview with the women playwrights demonstrated, the male domination of theatre. For example, Nell Dunn's all-female cast (with the exception of one unseen male presence) in her commercially successful play *Steaming*, performed shortly before *Top Girls* in 1981, and which sets the women in a Turkish bath, combines a bourgeois-feminist position with the dominant form of stage realism. By contrast, *Top Girls* exceptionally combines theatrical inventiveness with a more hard-hitting, radical political viewpoint which, rather than support mainstream, bourgeois feminism, takes issue with it.

From a socialist-feminist viewpoint the spectatorial experience of *Top Girls* is an important one. As feminist historian Rosalind Miles, commenting on the major British revival of *Top Girls* in 1991, observed and cautioned:

> Superb parts for women then, written by women – watching this on International Women's Day, a moment here and there felt like a new dawn. And yet. How much has changed for women in the theatre in the last nine years? Or in life? In *Top Girls*, the women trapped in traditional roles face a cruelly bleak future.[56]

The future remains as 'cruelly bleak' for those women in the 1990s as it did in the Thatcherite years of the 1980s, which were 'stupendous' for one class, but not for another. The need for Churchill's socialist-feminist critique of class and gender issues is arguably, therefore, all the more critical in the current backlash[57] climate of the 1990s when even the acceptable face of bourgeois feminism is under threat.

With *Cloud Nine*, Churchill achieved transatlantic and commercial success. *Top Girls*, similarly, was acclaimed in Britain and America. Both plays won Obie awards and went on to be performed around the world.[58] Churchill's success – and continued success – is due in part to her willingness to experiment (see chapter 5). In *Top Girls*, for example, it was the pleasure of the overlapping dialogue, additional to the techniques of doubling and time-shifting that she 'played' with in *Cloud Nine*, which caught the critical attention. Paying tribute to Churchill, Gillian Hanna has described her as 'the only woman I know of who has managed to keep herself at a level of enquiry... into the aesthetic process. She is constantly re-writing herself'.[59] The innovative approach of the 'woman writer' to theatre-making, the ability to 'constantly re-writ[e] herself', has secured Churchill a place not only in the canon of contemporary women's theatre which, regretfully, continues to occupy a marginal position in relation to dominant theatre and culture, but also in the 'malestream' of the modern British stage.[60]

3

The Dramatist as
Socialist Critic

I think labels and terms like feminist writer or woman writer or left-
wing writer vary very much...depending on who's using them and
why...I think I only mind it in any sense at all – and mostly I would
embrace it as being a reasonably accurate description – ...if you
think that in the other person's mind that conveys something very
narrow or specific which doesn't really cover the breadth of your
work, or that it conveys with it a stereotype of the kinds of things
that they expect that you'll be writing.[1]

Churchill has identified 'two obsessions' in her early work: one,
which was the focus of the opening chapter, was concerned with
'mental states, lovesickness, schizophrenia, and so on', and the
other was an 'anticapitalist, state of England sort of thing, usually
in a rather negative and sad mode'.[2] *The Ants*, Churchill's first
professional radio production (1962), described as 'the most
successful of these political plays',[3] illustrates this second
obsession.

The Ants uses a familial setting to dramatize an estranged set
of parents arguing over the custody of their son, Tim, who is
temporarily staying with his grandfather until marital dishar-
mony and living arrangements are resolved. As a refuge from
parental quarrelling, Tim focuses on a community of ants, but as
tempers flare he turns on the ants, and, finally, joins his
grandfather in setting fire to them:

Pour a little petrol on them, that's right. Now we put the string here
in the petrol and bring the end way over here so we can shelter from
the blast all right? Down we crouch, then, oh. Now we light the
string, here, see, light the string. [*He strikes a match.*] You take the
match, you do it. That's right. Blow out the match. Now you wait, the

46

string will burn all the way down to the enemy, see the little flame go all the way down to the ants.[4]

The radio play ends with the directions 'the petrol explodes into flame' and Tim 'shrieks with laughter'.[5] Metaphorically, the burning of the ants is designed to express the horrors of war, and the ways in which people (Tim) can switch from identifying with a community of people (the ants) to bombing (setting fire to) them. In this context, the damaging (emotionally violent) familial relationships are seen to give rise to an act of violence.

During the 1970s, the early political impulse of a piece like *The Ants* can be seen evolving in Churchill's dramatizations of an anti-capitalist stance, the exploration of violent actions, and strategies of social control and resistance. These emerge along-side, or, rather, are integral to the concerns of the 'woman writer'. As the opening quotation suggests, 'left-wing' and 'feminist' are both labels frequently used to describe Churchill's writing. Where the previous chapter foregounded Churchill as a feminist playwright, the purpose of this chapter is to look more closely at formative work which has contributed to her reputation as a left-wing writer; to bring her emergent role as socialist critic into focus.

'TERRORISM AND SEASIDE': *OBJECTIONS TO SEX AND VIOLENCE*

The issue of bombing, alluded to in *The Ants*, was one which Churchill returned to in her mid-1970s stage play *Objections to Sex and Violence* (1975). *Objections to Sex and Violence* was her next full-length production at the Court after *Owners*, although, before then, she had completed the writing of another play, *Moving Clocks Go Slow*, a science-fiction drama given a one-night performance later in 1975 in the Royal Court Theatre Upstairs.[6] Performed on the Court's main stage, *Objections to Sex and Violence* raised, as Churchill explained in her afterword to the play, published ten years after its production, 'immediate and pressing ideas about the anarchism, revolution and violence' in Britain in the early 1970s. She added that many of the IRA bombings had not happened at the time she wrote the piece, although 'it's hard to unthink them and see the play without them' (*OSV* 52).

Violence as an act of insurrection on the part of the individual is dramatized in the representation of the central female character, Jule. In Act One it is established that Jule has been living among a small group of agitators who are apparently prepared to use violence in protests against society. Although there are vague references to capitalism, revolution, and explosive devices, particular political affiliations, causes and the exact nature of intended violence are never clearly established. Reviewer Harold Hobson opined that the 'play's foundation... is the power, and especially the obscurity of the motives of violence'.[7]

The dramatic action is set on a beach where Jule and Eric, also a group member, are living in a tent following police raids and arrests made on conspiracy charges.[8] The issue of violence or more specifically objections to it, are raised through the dialogue between Jule, her sister Annie, and Annie's boyfriend Phil. Out of concern for Jule's safety, Annie and Phil have come looking for her at the seaside:

> JULE: What did you come for?
> ANNIE: You sent me a postcard.
> JULE: I didn't say come. I was keeping in touch.
> ANNIE: I read about the trouble in the paper, but when I took a train up you'd vanished. You weren't just out because I waited all day. The police said they hadn't kept you.
> JULE: It's not my fault you waited all day. I can't always be where you might drop in.
> ANNIE: So when I knew from the postmark you were here, I came here, that's all.
>
> (*OSV* 13)

Jule's subversive position in relation to violence is the catalyst for debating the morality of violent actions, and for looking at the violence people are subjected to in their everyday lives. Some of the most poignant moments in Act One, for example, centre on the gradual unfolding of Annie's story about her private and public life, at home and at work, which includes detail of a violent, past marriage and her inability to cope with her job as a secretary. Annie's monologue describing her work experience is a precursor to the narratives of disempowerment voiced by the interviewees in the *Top Girls* agency:

I was secretary to a top executive. But you know how it is. I go to pieces. They bust me down to the typing pool for a rest, they were quite concerned. That's when I should have left. But I like to feel committed. I don't know how to keep my distance. I bring my work home in my head as if it was interesting. As if I was competing like the men. You'd love the men, Jule, you'd laugh so much. You can tell the grade of a man by his car. The company provide them with different sizes so there's no mistaking who's important. (*OSV* 14)

Annie goes on to tell how she switched from office work to cleaning for her former boss, whom she admits to blackmailing after he desired to have sex with her on a regular basis. The day before coming away to find Jule, Annie had told her boss it was all over: 'I'm sick of blackmailing you all this time, it makes me feel ill' (*OSV* 25). He, however, then revealed that his wife had known about them all along, and had agreed to the sex and to the money. Annie's fantasy of being less of a victim of feeling that she 'was doing something to them' is destroyed:

I really thought I was doing something to them. I used to feel good cleaning up her shit because I thought I knew what was what and she'd got no idea. When really I was the one. That's all it is. Whatever you do to them, they can afford it, they include it, they glide. That's all it is that makes me cry. (*OSV* 26)

Although Jule tries to incite Annie to violent retaliation, suggesting a brick through the couple's window, Annie is forced to admit that, unlike her sister, she is unable to occupy an 'extreme position' (*OSV* 26).

Incitement to and resistance of subversive attitudes to sex and violence create the tensions in the drama, as Jule tries to persuade those around her of her views. Although the play is conventionally organized into two acts, there are moments when Churchill shows signs of experimenting with a more Brechtian style to demonstrate the issues of sex and violence as, for example, in the close of Act One when Annie, Jule and Phil are all roused to anger over the behaviour of Annie's employer. As in *The Ants*, lighting a fire creates a *Gestus* for upset, resentment and anger, and Jule's final line of the act, addressed to Annie, invites her not to 'turn away from it' (*OSV* 33). Similarly, Jule's anger with Eric in the second act, as he reveals he has half-promised the police information on the group members and is going to leave altogether in order to keep his silence, is imaged in the throwing of sand, and then the throwing of stones which becomes increasingly more violent and threatening.

After Eric retreats from the scene, Jule begins to bury herself in the sand, and, subsequently, Annie takes up the task of burying her sister until only her head is left showing. Reviewer W. Stephen Gilbert, while critiquing the play for its lack of 'visual realisation of the verbal motifs' described this 'decapitation' sequence as 'the most theatrical image of the evening':

> Annie has rendered Jule a talking head by burying her up to the neck in the sand, as she used to do in childhood. Mocked for her threat of violence, she stuffs sand in Jule's mouth and flounces off. The image is a small miracle of compression and evocation. Jule is, as it were, raped and murdered.[9]

Ultimately, although Jule is able to incite those around her to momentary anger they counter with objections of reasonableness. It becomes impossible, therefore, for Jule to establish a group dedicated to revolutionary violent action. One of Churchill's sources for *Objections to Sex and Violence* was Hannah Arendt's *On Violence* (*OSV* 52). In her study, Arendt, quoting from Frantz Fanon, explains the bonding which underpins 'collective violence':

> We find a kind of group coherence which is more intensely felt and proves to be a much stronger, though less lasting, bond than all the varieties of friendship, civil or private. To be sure, in all illegal enterprises, criminal or political, the group, for the sake of its own safety, will require 'that each individual perform an irrevocable action' in order to burn his bridges to respectable society before he is admitted into the community of violence.[10]

What Churchill shows in her drama is that neither Annie, Phil, Eric, nor Terry, Jule's estranged husband who turns up at the close of Act Two, can commit themselves to an 'irrevocable' violent action which would bind them to Jule's position and to a 'community of violence'.

Interwoven with this serious discussion of violence are scenes depicting 'the seaside couple Madge and Arthur' which are in a lighter comic vein (*OSV* 52). In her notes Churchill found a topical reference to the couple as follows: 'Mary Whitehouse and man in raincoat as married couple – both with same ashamed attitude to sex – they think of themselves as different but in fact identical' (*OSV* 52). In the early 1970s, objections to sex, or rather to representations of sex, were being raised by, for example, Mary Whitehouse's Viewers and Listeners Association, which paid fastidious attention to sex and media broadcasting, and Lord Longford's *Report on Pornography* published in 1972. Just as the other characters repress their momentary violent urges in the interests of civilized behaviour, Madge and Arthur repress sex and sexual fantasies as something shameful and disgusting, but to comic effect. Arthur, for example, lusts after Miss Forbes, another lonely, distressed figure who has come to the seaside, driven by a repressed past romantic memory. His advances towards Miss Forbes are en-acted in the postcard-cartoon style of a raincoat-flasher on the beach:

> ARTHUR: My wife disapproves of everything. I'm forced to go to shops for literature. I can't help it, it's a natural urge, it's disgusting but I can't help that. You're the same, you're no better, you dance, you've had men, you like it, you like it, you'd like it now, you want me to do it now, it's not my fault, you're making me do it, you're making me.
> *Arthur undoes his trousers.*
> touch me, quick, touch me, touch me, touch me –
> *Miss Forbes shrieks and rushes away. She trips over some rocks near the sea's edge and falls heavily.*
> *Arthur hastily does up his trousers.*
> Look what you made me do. It's not my fault. It's you. It should be stopped.
>
> (*OSV* 43)

Writing the afterword in the mid-1980s, Churchill stated that the title of her play suggested 'a different set of ideas, developed by feminists, of the links between male sexuality and violence, which wasn't my starting point at all' (*OSV* 52). This was a line of interpretation, however, which inflected Irving Wardle's (critical) reviewing of the original production, stating as he did that 'we are back in the traditional feminine world where personal relationships are all and everything would work out satisfactorily if men would only behave properly'.[11] 'With the possible exception of Terry, the communist husband', he continues, 'each of the men makes his exit with a knife from the author quivering between the shoulder blades'.[12] These comments, however, say more about the male bias and attitude of the reviewer than they do about the play. Although Churchill places a woman centre stage as the active protagonist, surrounded by relatively passive men (as she does, for example with Marion in *Owners)* there is little in the text of the drama itself to support the radical-feminist, anti-male position Wardle reads into the production.

Although the title may, as Churchill writing in 1985 suggested, signal issues of male-authored violence against women, a more topical concern for a revival of the play in the 1990s would probably be the relationship of women to violence. This has proved a controversial issue for feminism, as plays and films such as *My Sister in this House* (1981), *A Question of Silence* (1982), or, more recently, *Thelma and Louise* (1991) and *Lesbians Who Kill* (1992), have shown, and is one which Churchill would explore in her mid-1980s play, *A Mouthful of Birds* (see Chapter 5).

Meanwhile, not all critics were as severe as Wardle. Harold Hobson wrote that the 'English Stage Company has acquired a dramatist of an exceptionally high order',[13] and although W. Stephen Gilbert had reservations about *Objections to Sex and Violence*, he concluded his review by favourably comparing Churchill with the established left-wing, political writer, Edward Bond:

> It [*Objections to Sex and Violence*] reminds me at times of the work of Edward Bond, by which I mean the highest praise. The sheer economy and resonance of Bond's stagecraft is unsurpassed amongst contemporary dramatists. Ms Churchill may be going to alter that assessment. At any rate, she's going to be a major dramatist.[14]

Despite this praise, I would argue that the relatively conventional structure of *Objections to Sex and Violence* and the focus on individual acts of (potential, rather than actual) insurrection make the play less interesting, both stylistically and politically, than Churchill's first Joint Stock production, *Light Shining in Buckinghamshire* (1976).

FROM HISTORY TO HISTORICIZATION: *LIGHT SHINING IN BUCKINGHAMSHIRE*

Like *Vinegar Tom*, which, as was previously noted, Churchill was writing in the same period, *Light Shining in Buckinghamshire* is set in the seventeenth century. Churchill's dramatization challenges the oversimplified version of the English civil war between Cavaliers and Roundheads by offering a more complex view of this period in English history when, in the middle part of the century, in fighting to overthrow the monarchy, it was, briefly, believed to be possible to revolutionize the oppressed lives of ordinary men and women. Politically, Churchill moves from the subversive potential of the individual without a clearly defined cause, to the rebellion of a society seeking economic and sexual freedoms, and, stylistically, shifts from realistic dialogue punctuated by stylized moments to a performance mode more fully informed by Brechtian techniques.

Light Shining in Buckinghamshire was Churchill's first encounter with Joint Stock's method of collective working. In the initial three-to-four-week period of workshopping, which was how work for a project began, the time was spent familiarizing the company with seventeenth-century history. This was rather a different experience to the subsequent *Cloud Nine* workshop, as director Max Stafford-Clark explained:

> *Light Shining in Buckinghamshire*...was about an experience very distant from us – Levellers, Ranters and ecstatic religion in the mid-17th century; the workshop brought it closer to us, made it more familiar, whereas *Cloud Nine* was about ourselves and things that were familiar to us, and the period of work actually distanced it.[15]

In the same interview, Stafford-Clark went on to argue that the writing and performance processes benefit from this kind of workshop experience, because the actors bring to it a level of 'creativity' and 'commitment' not usually demanded of them:

> Actors are often in a situation where they make the most of what they've got. Their creativity is rarely called upon. You gain their commitment if you say to them: 'The script will finally be written by the author, but first we all have an opportunity to explore our own obsessions and create things from scratch, to explore, to initiate subjects'. You're tapping a source of energy that normally plays don't demand.[16]

Just as Churchill was excited by the collaborative, feminist project with Monstrous Regiment, working with Joint Stock was also a stimulating introduction to a new way of working and a departure from her more 'solitary' life as a writer. Her write-up of the *Light Shining in Buckinghamshire* project which she contributed to Rob Ritchie's *The Joint Stock Book* recaptures the 'thrill' of this new collective process and gives an insight into the kinds of improvization techniques which Joint Stock used:

> I'd never seen an exercise or improvisation before and was as thrilled as a child at a pantomime. Each actor had to draw from a lucky dip of bible texts and get up at once and preach, urging some extraordinary course of action justified from the Bible: 'Suffer little children to come unto me' became an impassioned plea to lay children in the street and run them over with a steamroller. They drew cards, one of which meant you were eccentric to the power of that number, and then improvised a public place – a department store, a doctor's waiting room – till it gradually became clear who it was, how they were breaking conventions, and how the others reacted.[17]

Churchill took away ideas, characters and scenes suggested to her during the workshopping period with Joint Stock, mixed with historical documentary sources, such as Leveller newspapers or Digger pamphlets. Close upon the rehearsal period, however, the script was still unfinished. A further drafting and exchange of ideas precipitated a shift from her concentration on six major roles, with actors playing minor parts in each others' narratives, to the concept of there being no continuity between actors and characters from scene to scene. This was jointly arrived at between Churchill and Stafford-Clark – first as a joke and then later as an idea to be taken seriously, as Churchill explains:

> We had the idea jointly – we suggested it jokingly, and then came back to it: 'What we ought to do is let everybody play different parts, and not worry about characters going through'. That reduced the number of scenes it needed, and it made everybody's experience seem shared. In a war or a revolution the same things happen to a lot of people. We then had to put it to the actors that they weren't going to play the parts they thought they were – they were all going to share the parts.[18]

While Churchill and Stafford-Clark were anxious about how the performers might react to the demands of sharing the parts, the collective distribution of roles and the radical break with the dramatic convention of actor-character identification was also one which made demands on the spectator. In his review, Irving

Wardle drew attention to the absence of 'personal heroes or villains', and, while describing the characterization of Cromwell as 'an affable negotiator' noted, in an aside, that this was observed 'on the one occasion he appears'.[19] Working against the tradition of actor-character identification, however, was central to making the play about ordinary people, and not – as Irving Wardle may have secretly liked – a historical play about Oliver Cromwell, for example. On the contrary, as David Zane Mairowitz argued, 'the play's history is rooted wholly in a collective consciousness which is its protagonist and hero', and although Mairowitz described the interchanging of roles as 'initially... confusing', he proceeded to argue that this was both theatrically and politically necessary:

> Churchill does not feel constrained by the pre-eminence of personality in our culture (and in our theatre), and twists our comprehension of inter-relationships in her view of events and in her operation of the stage. The brilliant collective playing of Joint Stock in Max Stafford-Clark's production first makes her style seem palatable, and finally correct and necessary.[20]

Writing and playing in a democratic, socialist, performance register enabled Churchill to ask different questions of seventeenth-century history; to demonstrate what is missing in the received, schools' version of English history. By playing in the 'gaps', Churchill and Joint Stock moved from a dramatic representation of history to a Brechtian mode of historicized performance. As feminist theatre scholar Elin Diamond explains in her seminal essay on 'Brechtian Theory / Feminist Theory', 'Brechtian historicization challenges the presumed ideological neutrality of any historical reflection'.[21] Diamond elaborates:

> In historicized performance, gaps are not to be filled in, seams and contradictions show in all their roughness, and therein lies one aspect of spectatorial pleasure – when our differences *from* the past and *within* the present are palpable, graspable, applicable.[22]

The dual movement between the historical past, and the present history-in-the-making is an important one. In both *Light Shining in Buckinghamshire* and *Vinegar Tom* it is not just a question of seeing the 'gaps' in seventeenth-century history but of also seeing them 'within the present'. Commenting on Brecht's 'disgust' with realism, because of its 'hegemonic' tendencies,

Diamond further adds that 'this is perhaps why the most innovative women playwrights refuse the seamless narrative of conflicting egos in classic realism'.[23] Neither *Light Shining in Buckinghamshire* nor *Vinegar Tom* offer 'seamless narratives' of individuals; rather, they are both rooted in collective representations which unpick the seams of history. Their respective collective performance registers democratize both the playing space and the playing of history.

Focusing more specifically on the dramatic text, it is possible to see how in *Light Shining in Buckinghamshire* Churchill moves from the individual as a member of a small, anarchic group, which she dramatized in *Objections to Sex and Violence*, to staging revolution, or rather, the possibility of revolution, on a national scale. As a socialist critic, she looks at the conditions which make a revolution possible, highlighting the failing authority of the king, the challenge to the integrity of government, and the willingness of the army to use force against the Royalists. However, the play also demonstrates the reasons behind the failed revolution. In the Putney debates which bring the first act to a close, it is property, ownership, i.e. developing capitalism, which Cromwell and his supporters use to argue against enfranchisement. In Act Two the betrayal of the people continues as the army, used to fighting for equality and freedom in God's name, is now armed against the Levellers and Diggers, and is used to fight against Ireland; the oppressed are forced to fight against the oppressed. In the final 'Meeting' scene, only the Ranters, with their faith in the millennium and the coming of Christ, remain clutching their hope of revolution before the Restoration.

Each scene in Churchill's Brechtian montage is a highly charged fragment of revolutionary belief, action and failure. As Irving Wardle explained, 'it is a model of expressive brevity, each scene, no matter how powerfully charged, cut off as if by a guillotine as the actor steps out of character'.[24] Civil battles and struggles are condensed and imaged through techniques of Brechtian reporting. Actors announce or narrate events, as in the opening to Act Two, for example, which documents the crushing of the Diggers, who tried to claim and work common land for the dispossessed poor, and, later in the act, the account of the funeral of Robert Lockyer, a Leveller leader, which is read by one of the actors from a Leveller newspaper (*P1* 228).

One of the key ways in which Churchill makes the complexities of this revolutionary moment in history accessible to the
spectator is through a recurrent imaging of the conflict between
those who can afford to eat and those who are forced to go
hungry. In Act One, for example, the vicar talks to his servant,
Claxton, while seated at a table set with wine (which he pours
only for himself) and oranges (*P1* 192–3). He preaches to Claxton
on greed as the cause of civil unrest and personalizes his
sermonizing by asking after Claxton's baby who is dangerously
ill. He brings their encounter to a close by offering Claxton an
orange from his table for the baby. The *Gestus* of the orange-
giving, discredits his (mis)understanding of a people who fight
not out of greed as he believes, but out of hunger and a need to
feed their families and to raise healthy children. His final
homily, 'And if it [the baby] is not spared, we must submit. We
all have to suffer in this life', is undercut by the direction '*He
drinks*' (*P1* 193). His rhetoric of godliness and caring for his
parishioners is demonstrated as nothing but self-interest and
self-importance.

Similarly, when the working man Briggs signs up for the
army, he simply looks on while the recruiting officer, Star, from
the mercantile classes, punctuates his explanation of the army's
Christian purpose with eating meat (*P1* 198-9). Despite arguing
social equality, Star reacts to the way in which Briggs marks their
'equal' standing by keeping his hat on in his presence. This,
therefore, undermines the sincerity of his explanations of social
and civil division, delivered in the manner of a Brechtian
teaching text designed to school Briggs in the distinction
between oppressors and oppressed; between Normans and
Saxons, and between Royalists and the army of Christ's saints.
Expanding on the culinary and biblical frame of reference used
by Star, Briggs recites his lesson back to his 'teacher':

BRIGGS: Bacon. Is bacon Norman?
STAR: Pork, Briggs. Pig. Very good.
BRIGGS: And Jacob the younger brother is the Saxon herds the pigs.
And Esau the older brother is the Norman eats the pork.
STAR: Very good, Briggs, Excellent.

(*P1* 199)

In Act Two, which strips away the possibility of revolution, being able to afford to eat is forcefully expressed in a scene showing a woman abandoning her baby because she cannot afford to feed it. This is positioned in between a scene in which Star is shown as the new landlord taking possession of the land, and proposing reforms for the so-called benefit of the poor, and a monologue in which a butcher addresses his (unseen) customers and threatens a gentleman customer who can afford to buy meat. The butcher's outburst is a violent and powerful imaging of the 'haves and have nots': 'You cram yourselves with their children's meat. You cram yourselves with their dead children' (*P1* 228). As rich men feed off the hunger of the poor, it is the poor and their children, and future generations of children, who are left starving. The sceptre of the child who is hungry and damaged by capitalist greed is an absent presence which haunts the action of the play (and future plays by Churchill, such as *Fen*, or, more recently still, *The Skriker*).

As the introduction of a capitalist system makes 'owners' of a few and beggars of many, it denies people the possibility of nourishment from the earth. In the final moments of *Light Shining in Buckinghamshire* the socialist dream of a more equal society is represented in the figure of Briggs, who is reduced to eating grass as he tries to balance the equation in which some eat too much by being someone who eats very little. But even when he forces his body to survive on grass alone, nevertheless, it is grass growing in a field which is owned by somebody else (*P1* 240).

Although gender is not a primary focus in *Light Shining in Buckinghamshire*, as it is in *Vinegar Tom*, ordinary women are shown to be more oppressed than men, both productively and reproductively. The figure of Margaret Brotherton, a displaced or dispossessed vagrant who is moved on from parish to parish, is representative of the ways in which women would increasingly have no sense of belonging in developing capitalism. In the Putney Debates it is only the enfranchisement of the common man which is debated, women are not considered. That women do not have a voice is further demonstrated when Hoskins tries to argue with the preacher who attempts to silence her with his pronouncement 'women can't speak in church' (*P1* 201). After Hoskins is beaten for trying to speak out, the wife of a working man tends her wounds and argues (with overtones of *Vinegar Tom)* the 'evil' and 'shameful' nature of women and their childbearing bodies as the rationalization for the silencing of women (*P1* 204). The invisibility of women is also highlighted in the scene 'Two Women Look in a Mirror' as the women see themselves for the first time in a mirror, left behind in the deserted house of a Royalist:

> 1ST WOMAN: There's an even bigger mirror that we didn't break. I'll show you where. You see your whole body at once. You see yourself standing in that room. They must know what they look like all the time. And now we do. (*P1* 207)

The possibility of working-class representation is, however, never realized – not for men, and especially not for women.

The exclusion of women from political and economic life, and the denial of sexual freedom, which women like Hoskins as a Ranter believed in, represent further 'gaps' for the feminist spectator to consider. The Women's Movement had its own war to wage on behalf of women's rights, but as Eva Figes was to caution in a revised edition of *Patriarchal Attitudes,* 'we are in danger of being lulled into a sense of premature complacency: we may have won the first battle, but we are still a long way from winning the war'.[25]

'WATCHING THE DETECTIVES': *SOFTCOPS*

Churchill continued her socialist critique in her work for television with *The After-Dinner Joke,* broadcast in 1978, which looked at capitalism and charity work.[26] The topic of terrorism and bombing surfaced again in *The Legion Hall Bombing* (1979) which took issue with the juryless Diplock Courts in Northern Ireland, and proved a controversial broadcast on account of last-minute censorship on the part of the BBC.[27] Immediately after this, Churchill worked on the scripting of *Softcops,* which she connects with *The Legion Hall Bombing* on account of the way in which both works tackle 'the depoliticization of crime, or calling things crimes that other people might call political acts'.[28]

For *Softcops,* Churchill acknowledges her debt to Foucault's *Discipline and Punish.* Taking her cue from Foucault, Churchill explores the evolution of social systems of control and punishment, and focuses on nineteenth-century France, setting the play in Paris during the 1830s. The spectator is taken through a series of scenes which explicate different methods of social control, from the spectacle of the tortured body to Bentham's Panopticon; from watching punishment to the punishment of being watched. Although Churchill wrote *Softcops* in 1978, it was not performed until Howard Davies's production of the play for the RSC in 1984. Michael Ignatieff described setting and set for the production as follows:

> *Softcops* is Foucault rendered as a music-hall turn and a Victorian freak-show, with music by Brecht and Gilbert and Sullivan. Set in the Paris of Vidocq and Lacenaire, the series of sketches is acted by an all-male company of players in dinner-jackets working on the bare boards of The Pit amid a set (by Bob Crowley) of draped mirrors, ladders doubling as gallows, tables and chairs doubling as execution blocks, and a hint of a Paris bordello in the middle distance. The Medici String Quartet plays by candle-light and offers mock-solemn musical shading for the action: a single plucked note to punctuate the silence of the Panopticon; a pizzicato in time with the boys scratching on their slates at the juvenile reformatory.[29]

By demonstrating how systems of social control operate and link up – the policing of education, punishment, mental health, and so on – Churchill shows how social behaviour is regulated and how, therefore, the power structure of government remains undiminished. Although there is no moment of revolution in *Softcops*, as dramatized in *Light Shining in Buckinghamshire*, the revolutionary impulse of *Softcops* lies in the spectator response to being shown how strategies of resistance are resisted by the enforcement of governmental power structures which seek to maintain law and social order. The spectator is, however, invited to question rather than accept the policing of social behaviour through understanding the mechanisms by which it is enforced. From the looking through to the being looked at sequences it is the spectator who is ultimately 'watching the detectives' and is empowered to interrogate the methods of 'softcop' control.

When the play was performed in 1984 it was the Panoptic principle of surveillance which caught the attention of audiences, given the association with George Orwell's 'Big Brother' (*P2* 3). Several of the reviewers, however, were unconvinced by and uncertain of what Churchill was attempting to portray in *Softcops*.

Criticisms varied from Rosalind Carne's damning 'one of the least enjoyable evenings I can remember in three years' regular theatre going... it keeps you guessing, and hoping, but consistently fails to provide what it promises',[30] to Michael Billington's more benign, 'I think I see what Ms Churchill is against, I am not sure what she is for'.[31]

The mode of looking in *Softcops* is directed by the figure of Pierre who functions as the spectator's link between each tableau of punishment. As the play opens, Pierre is stage-managing his organized spectacle of punishment. To an audience of invited schoolchildren he explains the theatrical sign-system of the scaffolding set for the 'performance'. As a semiotician, Pierre has worked to determine the scenic encoding and to direct and close off meanings. The impossibility of this task, however, is highlighted as he makes last-minute set changes; for example, having the red ribbons, which he wants the children to 'read' as symbols of blood and passion, removed because they intrude too much on the black of the scaffolding drape, signifying grief. Moreover, the scripting of roles which he has so carefully prepared goes wrong as his 'cast' of prisoners and local dignitaries forget their lines and have to be prompted. Pierre's performance is a complex indexing of Brechtian theatre – a performance designed to make the children think, where scenes are announced by placards (which Pierre gets wrong), and actors break the fourth wall convention, stepping in and out of character – which has dangerous consequences for the actor-prisoners who 'play' with their 'real' bodies. Ultimately, Pierre's inability to semiotically determine the meaning of his performance is demonstrated in the crowd response to the murderer Lafayette, whose refusal to deliver his rehearsed speech of contrition and his expression of pleasure in having killed his boss, incites a riot. In this brief moment of insurrection it is the crowd who becomes the performer and controls the 'spectacle'.[32] Order is restored, however, by using soldiers, indicating, as was shown in *Light Shining in Buckinghamshire,* that the allegiance of an armed force is crucial to establishing and maintaining, or to bringing down, structures of governmental power.

Brechtian styled role-playing continues in the 'cop and robber' sequence which follows, depicting Vidocq, arch villain turned Chief of Police and Lacenaire, who, as Churchill explains, was a 'glamorous and ineffectual murderer and petty thief, who was briefly a romantic hero' (*P2* 3). The Brechtian, multi-disguised, multiple-role-playing of Vidocq and the interchange-ability of villain and cop identities makes ambiguous the demarcation between law enforcement and criminality, while the circus-style celebration of Lacenaire is used for political ends to conceal the more dangerous figure of Fieschi, put to death for trying to kill the king (*P2* 32). Ideologically, this is a clear example of what Churchill wanted to show as the representation of a political act as a crime.[33] Stylistically, as one critic described, the overall effect was 'a cross between the *Marat/Sade* and the more arid Mr Bond'.[34]

Vidocq's control of crime (and it is now crimes against property which is seen as the major issue), poses a problem for Pierre. Catching criminals is all very well he admits, but what happens 'if you don't use their bodies to demonstrate the power of the law' (*P2* 30). Foucault asks a related question of his theoretic in *Discipline and Punish*, as he queries the framing of his study, which traces the way in which the visible body as the si[gh]te of punishment was displaced by systems of correction which addressed the unseen 'soul' of the transgressor, against a background of 'a history of bodies'. However, as the more adept semiotician, Foucault recognizes that 'even when they use "lenient" methods involving confinement or correction, it is always the body that is the issue – the body and its forces, their utility and their docility, their distribution and their submission'.[35] Moreover, it is the body as sign-system he goes on to explain, which is 'directly involved in a political field; power relations have an immediate hold upon it; they invest it, mark it, train it, torture it, force it to carry out tasks, to perform ceremonies, to emit signs'.[36] Pierre, through understanding Bentham's Panoptic principle, is eventually persuaded of the effectiveness of a system of punishment which shifts from visibility to invisibility; from the spectacle of the 'theatre' to the power 'machine' of surveillance (*P2* 40). Michael Ignatieff describes the theatrically effective enactment of the Panoptic principle in the 1984 production:

> Bentham explains the Panopticon. He drapes a ladder with a shroud, places a bowler hat on top of it and disappears behind. Silence

descends, the prisoner stares at the ladder, we stare at the ladder, and it begins to stare back at us. Quick as a wink, Bentham appears behind the prisoner's back, smiling benignly at his terror. It's not being watched that matters, it's thinking you're being watched.[37]

It is the *Gestus* of the marked body, however, which Churchill uses to make the repressed traces of social control visible: the children in their harnesses of physical and spiritual correction; the 'docile' bodies of the young boys in 'family' institutions of correction, and the 'rehabilitated' bodies of Pierre's hospital patients in the final scene.

Given that when performed in 1984 *Softcops* had an all-male cast, critical readings have sometimes separated this play from Churchill's emergent feminism. Jane Thomas, for example, states that 'Churchill's anonymous group of males is presumably representative of all deviations from the bourgeois norm including non-whites and women', and goes on to argue that 'gender did not constitute a focus for her [Churchill's] ideas until the late seventies'.[38] This, however, overlooks the complex interconnections of feminism and politics in Churchill's theatre in the 1970s, and, moreover, specifically negates the gender focus of *Vinegar Tom*, written in 1976 before the writing of *Softcops* in 1978.

The idea that the men in the play represent or stand in for women is, however, an important one. Janelle Reinelt, offering a different view than that of Thomas, sees the absence of women in the play as having 'profound implications for the feminist project', stating that, 'women do not have to be represented on the stage for a gender critique to take place or for a feminist politic to underlie the dramaturgy'.[39] Systems of patriarchal control in which women have no place is, therefore, as Reinelt proposes, highly relevant to feminist concerns. The absence of women in the realm of the symbolic points to the patriarchal control and 'softcop' policing of social, political, cultural and theatrical sign-systems.

In brief, this shows how hard it is to separate Churchill's politics from her feminism. One might easily, for example refigure the discussion of *Owners* through the socialist lens of this chapter, and, similarly, it is impossible not to come back to the feminist impulse which inflects the socialist concerns of the plays studied in this chapter.

4

Communities in Dramatic Dialogue

Research has always been important to Caryl Churchill's theatre-making. In prefaces, introductions, afterwords and interviews where she discusses her work, Churchill cites sources and publications which have helped to shape her drama, and, in this way, she permits the reader access to the thinking and making process of her work and ideas.[1] Additionally, she also acknowledges her debt to group work, with companies such as Monstrous Regiment and Joint Stock, as detailed in the previous two chapters, and to directors, designers, and so on, who have collaborated with her in the theatrical process.

Research and the sharing of ideas underpin the three plays studied in this chapter in a special kind of way: they are all projects which involved Churchill, and the company she was working with, in oral research with particular communities. The first of these, *Fen* (1983), was researched by Joint Stock out in a remote East Anglian fen village. *Serious Money* (1987) took Churchill and actors from the Royal Court into London's world of high finance, and *Mad Forest* (1990) involved her and students from the Central School of Speech and Drama in a field-trip to Romania to grapple with political upheaval in Eastern Europe. All three projects relied on meeting with and engaging in dialogue with people involved in each community, whether in East Anglia, London, or Bucharest.

'LAND-GIRLS': *FEN*

In 1983, the year of *Fen*'s production, Mary Chamberlain published a revised edition of her collection of interviews,

Fenwomen, which documents the experiences of girlhood, schooling, marriage, work, religion, politics, recreation and ageing of women in a Fen village.[2] Churchill acknowledges her debt to this study (from which she took quotations for the 'Girls' Song' in Scene Seven),[3] but, like Chamberlain, she and Joint Stock, also conducted their own oral research. Through talking to people, the actors learned about the lives, the work, and the history of the Fen community. As Chamberlain explains, researching orally in this way, the representation of 'people's words and memories' are 'not the silent labours of a solitary archivist, but the result of a dialogue'.[4] Moreover, she argues that researching oral history 'offers the possibility of creating a democratic history in that it offers the means of expression for the past of the "common people" and offers a participation in that process'.[5] *Fen* is 'the result of a dialogue' with a community, and, arguably, demonstrates Churchill using theatre to stage 'democratic history', as she did in *Light Shining in Buckinghamshire*.

Churchill has described *Fen* as the 'most documentary' of her Joint Stock projects,[6] noting that '*Fen* is a play with more direct quotes of things people said to us than any other I've written' (*P2* ix). During the period of research, the actors would not record or write down what people said to them, but would go back to the company to present a person they had met to the group.[7] Out of this material Churchill devised a cast of twenty-two characters originally shared between a company of six performers. Reviewing the production, Michelene Wandor criticized the researching and workshopping method for the way in which it was 'reflected in the structure of the piece – a large number of characters representing as many different types of people as can be crammed in'.[8] However, like *Light Shining in Buckinghamshire* or *Vinegar Tom*, as a representation of 'democratic history' the emphasis in *Fen* is on the portrait of a collective rather than the individual; on the representation of a community of ordinary, oppressed people.

The community in *Fen* is largely, although not exclusively, represented by different generations of women who are shown working the land and looking after their homes and children. It is portrayed as a never-ending cycle of drudgery and oppression, passed on from generation to generation; from mothers to daughters. The monotony of the work cycle is imaged in Scene

Two, for example, which shows the women working out in a potato field. Churchill's directions state that they work *'in a row...When their buckets are full they tip the potatoes into a potato grave at the top of the field'* (P2 148). The young women in the community may have their aspirations, as Churchill represents in the lyrics of the 'Girls' Song', but ultimately their dreams do not take them beyond the village which binds them to harsh work on the land, early marriages and child-rearing: 'I want to be a nurse when I grow up/ And I want to have children and get married./ But I don't think I'll leave the village when I grow up' (P2 157). The future for them, as for Angie in *Top Girls*, is 'frightening'. It is through the theatricalization of the ordinary lives of the Fenwomen that the documentary style which Churchill argues for *Fen* is clearly illustrated. Compare Churchill's dramatic documentation, for example, with this brief extract from a factual account of 'Everyday Life of the Fen':

> One of the factors is inherent to the fens and it is an attitude of fear; 'better not step out of line or the employer will have me out'. This is obviously the result of many years hard work and exploitation. Also the fens are very much closed village communities with little opportunity for employment. Even if the girl does receive a decent education and is encouraged to take it seriously there will be very limited job opportunities at the end of it. Therefore the only way to get a good job is to move out of the area and again the fen attitude tends to want not to leave their home village and family.[9]

The cycle of oppression is reinforced in *Fen* by the central figure of Val, who attempts but fails to resist her social destiny. She tries to escape to London with her two daughters and her lover, Frank, but stays tied to the village, recognizing that they do not have the work skills to survive in the city. In order to be with Frank, Val has to give up her daughters. Scene Four, which shows her leaving the children, undercuts the transitory moment of happiness in a wordless Scene Five, in which Val and Frank are seen dancing together: *'Old-fashioned, formal, romantic, happy'* (P2 153). Romance was not something which, as Mary Chamberlain's research revealed, Fenwomen experienced as part of their lives:

> Romance and glamour – the opium of women – had, they felt, passed the fen by. For life on the land is neither romantic nor glamorous. Just hard work, in uncompromising weather, in rough

old working clothes padded out with newspaper against the wind. Small chance to catch a young man's fancy. Marriage for convenience or marriage to conform, particularly for the older women. Then back to the soil. Land worker, home servicer.[10]

When Val is shunned by her community for leaving her children in pursuit of romance and happiness, she takes refuge in religion, which turns out to be a farcical sham of sisterly bonding and comfort, and, ultimately, finding that she can neither live with Frank without her children, nor be with her children without Frank, she invites her lover to kill her as the only means of escaping.

Each time Val turns to women in her family or in her community of friends for help, they preach acceptance rather than resistance. As Shirley, a field-worker and fifty-year-old grandmother counsels, 'You've too much time on your hands. You start thinking. Can't think when you're working in the field can you?' (P2 168). Women like Val, who want to change the oppressive patterning of their lives are seen as deviant, are represented as misfits by their community. Nell, for example, who is one of the few women to protest her rights as a worker (P2 150, 180), is taunted by the village girls for her 'morphrodite' body (P2 155), and Shirley's rebellious granddaughter Sukey is singled out for comment because of her green hair. Val argues, 'Sukey's a freak round here but if she went to a city she wouldn't be, not so much', adding, 'And I wouldn't' (P2 168).

Val, who doubles with the ghost of a nineteenth-century mother and farm-worker whose 'baby died starving' (P2 163), and the generations of women dramatized alongside her, represent the silenced history of the Fenwomen. As one reviewer explained, 'the mothers, daughters and granddaughters whose voices the play amplifies serve as a Greek chorus for a hitherto silent pageant of female emotion'.[11] The focus on the women as representative of the Fen community is significant because it is the women who are doubly oppressed, by their class and by their gender. The ties that bind them to the village, as Val discovers, are financial as well as familial. The double oppression of work and domesticity was visually represented in the set for the original production, for which designer Annie Smart created a field as the 'floor' to both exterior and interior scenes. The presence of the flat, bleak, landscape of the fens further served as a visual counterpoint to the linguistic register of dreams, romance, and story-telling which the women use as a means of 'escape', illustrated, for example, in Angela's dream of living in the 'romantic' rural landscape of the Lake District (P2 181), or Nell's diversionary tale of passion and murder (which prefigures Val's 'murder'), narrated while the women pack onions into boxes (Scene Ten).

Class and gender oppression are also encoded in the ensemble style of playing which Churchill's text invites. The one male performer in the original Joint Stock production, who was assigned four character roles, had to play both the oppressed farm-worker and the landowning farmer, thereby marking the discourse of oppressor and oppressed on and through his body. This is highlighted in Scene Three when the actor playing Frank mimes working on a tractor as he carries on a dialogue with Tewson, the farmer: Frank argues in favour of higher wages, while the farmer argues against him. The split-subject dialogue is visually underlined in the gestural encoding of oppressor and oppressed as Frank hits Tewson, that is, '*he hits himself across the face*' (P2 151). Similarly, Scene Six stages an oppressor and oppressed relationship between a stepmother, Angela, and her stepdaughter, Becky. The violent nature of their relationship is gesturally represented by Angela forcing Becky to drink a cup of very hot water, while Angela taunts Becky about her absent, dead mother. The absence of the real mother, who signifies comfort and security, and the reality of the stepmother, who represents violence and danger, are gesturally marked in the dual movement from 'good' to 'bad' mother at the close of the scene, as '*Angela strokes Becky's hair then yanks it*' (P2 154).

A feel for the violence in the Fen community, and a history of violence in the Fens, such as the nineteenth-century food riots, came out of the oral research. Churchill noted that discontent in the community was the kind that turned itself into aimless violence, rather than being channelled in a political direction.[12] *Fen* illustrates the little impact which the political activities of the union, past and present, have had in improving the lives of ordinary workers. The recollections of Fenwoman Ivy on her ninetieth birthday narrate the generations of landowners in the Tewson family who intimidated the workers to try and prevent them joining the unions:

Fellow come round on his bike and made his speech in the empty street and everybody'd be in the house listening because they daren't go out because what old Tewson might say. 'Vote for the blues, boys,' he'd say and he'd give them money to drink. They'd pull off the blue ribbons behind the hedge. Still have the drink though. (P2 177–8)

In the present, scenes of the women working the fields for a nineteenth-century style of gangmaster, empowered to hire, fire and set the level of wages, demonstrate their exploitation and lack of job security or employment rights (Scenes Two and Twelve). By making the gangmaster a woman, Churchill demonstrates, as she does in *Top Girls*, that it is not just men who abuse women from a position of power. Exploitation is further underlined by the juxtaposition of, for example, Scene Two with Scene One which opens with a Japanese Businessman assigned a monologue detailing the history of capitalist investors in the fens. In the present, landowners like Tewson, selling out to city investors because of taxes on the land (see Scene Nine), perpetuate the history of the capitalist cycle of exploiters and exploited.

Val's 'murder' at the close of the play marks a shift in register from sparse realism to a surreal discourse which links past and present suffering in a resistant vision of fen misery. Angela, who inflicts pain on Becky to anaesthetise her own misery is made to feel her own pain. Nell is seen striding out on stilts like her ancestors who rebelled against the draining of the Fens. Shirley, whose class and gender oppression is imaged in the sight of her ironing the field, remembers what it feels like to be unhappy. The boy from the last century who scares the crows crosses the landscape. Finally, Val's mother May, who would never sing because she could never fulfil her dream of becoming a singer, sings. This is not a utopian realization of her dream, but a recognition of missed opportunity, signalled in the closing Brechtian *Gestus* of May *'stand[ing] as if singing'*, as the spectator hears *'what she would have liked to sing'*, in the form, as Churchill notes for the original production, of *'a short piece of opera on tape'* (P2 145) The dislocation between the voice of the singer and the recorded song signifies the gap between harsh social reality and beautiful dream.

'MONEYSPEAK': *SERIOUS MONEY*

While *Fen* focused on the rural working-class community in East Anglia, *Serious Money* looked at the rise of working-class money-makers in London's changing world of high finance. To research the project, Churchill, Max Stafford-Clark and performers from the Court 'made daily observational forays to the trading floors and dealing rooms of the City', and, as with *Fen*, the performers 'then re-enacted their experiences... in an attempt to create a "work-study" of a community'.[13] This introduced them to the changing practices of the Stock Exchange, engaged them in dialogue with the new 'barrow boy' traders, and taught them the new language of 'serious moneyspeak', 'the current City slang'.[14] As actress Linda Bassett commented, they met people, most of whom seemed to be aged about 23, who were earning between £40,000 and £50,000, when the performers were, at that time, working for a wage of about £130 a week.[15] After the workshopping in the autumn of 1986, Churchill took the research away, spent several months engrossed in the *Financial Times,* before rehearsals and, finally, in March 1987, the production of her 'City comedy' took place. Unlike *Fen's* sympathetic portrait of an oppressed community, *Serious Money* emerged as a satirical critique of the greed and corruption driving the London money markets, and, by implication and association, the Conservative government.

Serious Money is a complex and amoral web of wheeling and (insider) dealing, where the money-makers sacrifice relatives, family, friends, and relationships to make a profit. The dramatic narrative is woven out of two criss-crossing threads: the death (murder?) of commercial paper dealer Jake Todd, and the bid by Billy Corman to take over the company Albion Products. Solving the enigma of Jake's death is the task of his sister Scilla, a LIFFE (London International Financial Futures Exchange) dealer, but she quickly becomes more interested in finding out about how Jake was making enormous sums of 'serious money', and, most importantly, where his money is being held, so that she can claim it for herself. Ultimately the precise cause of Jake's death remains unsolved – although the involvement of the British government, MI5, or the CIA, is hinted at (*P2* 305).

Scilla's investigative drive connects the Albion bid to Jake as she retraces his life through his diary, which contains not events (there's no time for socializing unless business combines with pleasure), but commercial contacts. Through the banker Zackerman (Zac), who supports Corman's bid for Albion, she gets to Corman, and, finally, to the American arbitrageur (a money market speculator), MaryLou Baines. It is Jake's trading in information, enabling speculators like Baines to make their money, which has aroused the suspicions of the DTI – helped by a 'phonecall from an embittered, old-fashioned stock exchange dealer, who is disillusioned with current trading 'standards'. The DTI investigation is, possibly, connected in some way with Jake's death, which, in turn, makes the transatlantic money markets reverberate with fear. As Zac describes, Jake is 'the kind of loose thread' that could make 'the whole fucking city ...unravel' (P2 256). (The same kind of fears arose in the 1990s when Nick Leeson's trading bankrupted Barings Bank and made the international money markets nervous.)

The action is condensed into the immediate aftermath of Jake's death, but mixing past and present is realized through flashback sequences, held together by Zac who functions as a narrative linking-device. Theatrically this demonstrates the corrupt money-making practices before and after the Big Bang deregulation of the Stock Exchange. As one critic described it, 'we are in a predatory world where the clubby corruption of the old City is being replaced by the wolfish greed of the deregulated Eighties'.[16] Moreover, Churchill opens her play with a scene from Thomas Shadwell's *The Volunteers, or The Stock-Jobbers*. The imaging of late-seventeenth-century trading among the mercantile classes, seeking to 'turn the penny in the way of stockjobbing' (P2 196), provides a historical example which underscores Churchill's critique of capitalism. As Janelle Reinelt summarizes 'the play's foundation, then, is the Brechtian historicization of finance'.[17]

Scilla and Jake are central not only to the dramatic organization of *Serious Money*, where Jake functions as an enigma and Scilla as investigator, but also to the play's class confrontation between the old boy network and the emergence of the 'barrow boys' in the money markets. Brother and sister are marked by the discourses of both classes: by their property-owning, middle-to-upper-class family, and the class of 'new market makers'. Jake is described by the uneducated dealer Grimes, who has one CSE in metalwork (*P2* 207), as 'the only public schoolboy what can really deal', which Jake claims is 'because I didn't go to university and learn to think twice' (*P2* 205).

As a woman, Scilla has twice offended her familial class: firstly, by going out to work, and, secondly, by going to work without 'being part of an old boy network' (*P2* 281). The warring class discourses are gesturally encoded in Scilla's dialogue precisely because she is a woman engaging in masculine power- and language-play. When, for example, Scilla insists that Zac call MaryLou Baines, so that she can finally make contact with the American speculator with a view to getting her hands on her brother's money, his surprise that she is not the 'English rose' he thought she was, is met with, 'go stick the thorns up your nose, bozo' (*P2* 295–6). And, when Scilla finally meets with MaryLou, she describes herself as a ruthless combination of having the 'cunning and connections of the middle class', while being as 'tough as a yob' (*P2* 305). As the LIFFE scenes at the close of Act One illustrate, women like Scilla who join the money-makers work in a sexist profession, and surviving means speaking the same language. The women use the same 'yob' language about the men as the men do about the women:

JOANNE: Do you call him Dick because he's got spots?
JILL: No, I call him Spot because he's a dick'.

(*P2* 24)

The power-play between the 'old boys' and the new 'barrow boys' is linguistically marked throughout the play. When, for example, the chairman of Albion (England) is under threat from Corman's take-over bid, the 'white knight' (someone who comes to the rescue of a company facing a hostile take-over bid) constructs an image of the company as a 'good old English firm'. In an Arthurian discourse of knights rescuing maidens from villains, Albion (England) is positioned as the maiden and potential rape victim of the villain, Corman (*P2* 235). (The artifice of this strategy is, however, immediately exposed by the white knight's switch from Arthurian imagery to his pragmatic 'we can talk about closing Scunthorpe later', *P2* 235.)

Corman also represents the take-over bid as a sexual act, but not in Arthurian terms, rather as a rapacious act of 'screwing'.

'Sexy greedy *is* the late eighties', argues the PR consultant trying to construct an image for Corman in his fight for Albion (*P2* 287). Screw others before they screw you is the ethos of the deregulated 1980s, and 'moneyspeak' is a language trading in sexual obscenities. To make money is, as Ian Dury's lyrics to the song which brings Act One to a close state, to 'do the fucking business' (*P2* 253). Moreover, 'Do[ing] the fucking business' leaves no time for the 'business of fucking', as comically illustrated in the inability of Zac and Jacinta Condor (a Peruvian business woman) in the second act, to find a 'window' for pleasure (sex).

Traders no longer buy and sell products, but deal in one commodity: money. As Scilla explains in a direct address to the audience: 'You can buy and sell money, you can buy and sell absence of/ money, debt, which used to strike me as funny' (*P2* 244). For economically deprived countries, the act of trading or speaking money is also an act of colonization as Western money markets profit at the expense of the Third World economy. Churchill demonstrates this in the representation of Jacinta, who is both colonized and colonizer. Coming from Peru, she belongs to a country of the oppressed, but money empowers her to colonize by trading in and with the West at the expense of her own nation. As her accomplice, Nigel Abjibala, states: 'One thing one learned from one's colonial masters,/ One makes money from other people's disasters' (*P2* 261). When researching the City, Churchill described how 'one of the actors . . . from St. Kitts, was astonished to see that the price of sugar, so important to his country's economy, was determined by what happened in a small room between a few listless young men'. She added, 'that was one of the moments when we could connect what we saw in the City with the world outside'.[18]

Moreover, the colonizing impulse may be read as under-pinning the ethos of the corrupt international money markets. Churchill resists any suggestion that the displaced old boys network was somehow morally better than the thoroughly amoral class of new marketeers. All of the characters in her dramatization of the world of high finance are dissolute and espouse the creed of 'do others before they can do you' (*P2* 305). It is the spectator who is positioned as the only potentially moral agent in the performance frame; who is invited through the Brechtian mode of address to cast a critical eye over the world of high finance.

However, reviewers noted that 'despite her [Churchill's] stern intentions, she makes the buccaneering atmosphere of the City seem rather attractive'.[19] Peter Lewis, commenting on the audiences at the Royal Court production, observed that 'at least two City firms booked the entire theatre to take their staff on a kind of Yuppie works outing'.[20] After the transfer to Wyndham's, Jeremy Kingston noted that 'the show's popularity among exactly the people it set out to condemn is one of its more intriguing features', adding that it was 'rather as though coachloads of Venetian Jews had driven up to applaud Mr Shakespeare's play about a vengeful Jewish usurer'.[21] Reported comments from City spectators seemed to indicate that they found it 'very true to life'.[22] In short, the verve of Churchill's writing combined with the high-energy mode of Joint Stock's physical performance style of ensemble playing enabled the spectator to experience the adrenalin, but not always, it would appear, her satirical view of the money market.

Drama scholar Ruby Cohn, while praising the 'demonic energy' of *Serious Money*, blames this failing on Churchill's use of verse, arguing that she finds the play 'hard . . . to take seriously as satire', because 'the energetic rhymes pound home the repetitive quality of corruption, unredeemed by any direct or honest statement'.[23] However, this overlooks the way in which Churchill's satirical purpose is clearly signalled in her verse, which she creates out of City slang and obscene 'moneyspeak', alien to the non-City spectator. The programme for the Wyndham's production, for example, included explanations of City scandals and glossaries of the City slang. While those inside the markets may easily read the signs encoded in the different coloured blazers (uniforms) of the traders and understand the language of 'moneyspeak', the non-City spectator is alienated by visual and linguistic sign-systems; is positioned as 'outsider', as critical observer.

Rather, audience reactions to *Serious Money* demonstrate that the dramatist – like the semiotician Pierre in *Softcops* – cannot 'fix' meaning or determine audience response. It further references the complex role of the spectator in the reception process; the spectator as active and acting participant in the production of meaning. If the spectator shares in the ethos of greed and corruption encoded in the performance text, she/he may engage in the pleasure of identification, refusing to 'see' the signs which position her or him as the satirical subject. For example, Ian Dury's second song which closes the play, 'Five More Glorious Years', critiques the 1987 Conservative re-election, heralding a possible further five years of greed and corruption. But the critique may not be 'heard' by those for whom Thatcher's re-election was a cause for celebration; who delighted in the prospect of being 'pissed and promiscuous', earning 'ridiculous' money for another five years (P2 308). Ironically, however, if Churchill's socialist critique was overturned in one way, it was served in another: the pleasuring of right-wing City audiences helped to make 'serious money' for left-wing theatre.[24]

'TWO WEDDINGS AND A REVOLUTION': *MAD FOREST*

Political systems of power and oppression constitute a dominant motif in *Mad Forest*, Churchill's dramatization of the 1989 Romanian revolution. Having worked with Churchill for Joint Stock, the then artistic director of Central, Mark Wing-Davey, proposed a Joint Stock Style of workshopping for this East European project. This resulted in taking British drama students out to Bucharest to stay with the families of Romanian students with whom they worked and researched. Again, much of the research for *Mad Forest* was conducted out on the street, talking to ordinary Romanian people.[25] For Churchill, taking students out to Romania to research this project was a way of 'working away from the mainstream' with young people who were 'the same age as the people who made the revolution'.[26]

The research trip to Romania took place just a few months after the fall of Ceausescu in December 1989, and therefore at a moment of post-revolutionary chaos as Romanian citizens were trying to take stock of what had happened and what the future held for them. While Churchill worked on *Mad Forest* for its production in June 1990, Romania was struggling to come to terms with the election of Illiescu and the National Salvation Front, associated with the old Ceausescu regime, and, as the play opened, students were again being subjected to violence as miners in Bucharest were brought in to crush anti-Front protesters. Some reviewers were critical of *Mad Forest* for failing to tackle this latest twist in events, although it is difficult to see how theatre can keep pace with the real life drama of events. Reviewer Benedict Nightingale offered a practical piece of advice: 'Churchill should keep *Mad Forest* in her word-processor, ready to up-date, revise. It could become one of her most striking plays'.[27]

Nightingale also had praise for the way in which the 'unfinished feel' of *Mad Forest* succeeded in capturing the real-life chaos of revolution and history in the making. The 'unfinished feel' is created through the dramatization of fragments from the lives of ordinary people – orally researched by the cast – from before, during and after the revolution. Two weddings frame this three-part structure, situated either side of the second, middle section which represents the revolution of December 1989. The first and third sections trace the lives of two families, one working class (the Vladu family) and one middle class (the Antonescu family), and the ways in which their lives are conditioned by the oppressive Ceausescu regime and post-liberation disorder. The Vladu family are especially affected in the opening section by the marriage of their daughter Lucia, to an American – a 'betrayal' which places the whole family under the surveillance of the secret police. Further tensions arise from this wedding, which concludes the first section, as it makes it difficult for the cross-class marriage between Lucia's sister Florina, and Radu, from the Antonescu family, to take place. The revolution is what makes the second wedding possible.

Where *Serious Money* uses the City language of 'moneyspeak' to drive the action on, *Mad Forest* shows people afraid to communicate, to act through speaking In Part One, revolution can only be whispered in meat-buying queues (*MF* 17), or joked about in low voices among trusted friends (*MF* 20–21). As people are afraid of how their own words might be used against them, familial conversation is either silenced or conducted only when the radio is turned up loud (*MF* 13). Bogdan's protest over the prospect of his daughter marrying an American is enacted visually rather than verbally: he smashes one of four eggs which Lucia offers to her family with her American cigarettes (*MF* 13).

(The egg is quickly salvaged by Bogdan's wife, Irina. It is too precious to waste.) Public speech is reserved for the praise of Ceausescu, as illustrated in the teacher, Flavia Antonescu, addressing her pupils in a monologue on the merits of the president (*MF* 16). Privately, however, a dialogue between Flavia and her dead grandmother, reveals the numbness she feels at living a lie; living a life that 'nobody's living' (*MF* 26). That Flavia's thoughts and feelings are shared with a figure who is already dead underlines the risks of speaking openly with the living. Similarly, a priest, seeking comfort from the danger of talking, holds a conversation with an Angel:

> This is so sweet, like looking at the colour blue, like looking at the sky when you're a child lying on your back, you stare out at the blue but you're going in, further and further in away from the world, that's what it's like knowing I can talk to you. Someone says something, you say something back, you're called to a police station, that happened to my brother. So it's not safe to go out to people and when you can't go out sometimes you find you can't go in, I'm afraid to go inside myself, perhaps there's nothing there, I just keep still. But I can talk to you, no one's ever known an angel work for the Securitate. (*MF* 21)

The gap or contradiction between what is said and what is unspoken is demonstrated in a scene in which Lucia asks a doctor for an abortion. The dialogue involves Lucia making her request and the doctor refusing her request, but, at the same time, they carry on a silent exchange of words (on paper) during which the abortion is agreed to and paid for:

DOCTOR: There is no abortion in Romania. I am shocked that you even think of it. I am appalled that you dare suggest I might commit this crime.
LUCIA: Yes, I'm sorry.
LUCIA gives the doctor an envelope thick with money and some more money.
DOCTOR: Can you get married?
LUCIA: Yes.
DOCTOR: Good. Get married.
The DOCTOR writes again, LUCIA nods.
DOCTOR: I can do nothing for you. Goodbye.
Lucia smiles. She makes her face serious again.
LUCIA: Goodbye.

(*MF* 19)

As Janelle Reinelt explains, 'these different Brechtian gests of talking (or not) enable the relationship between communication and ideology to become visible'.[28]

The Brechtian style of *Mad Forest* is structurally encoded in the three-part montage of scenes, captioned with titles announced in Romanian and English. As Churchill instructs that a performer reads these titles in the manner of an English tourist using a Romanian phrase book (*MF* 13), the difficulty of expression is again underlined. In Part Two, one is forcefully reminded of Brecht's revolutionary street scene in *The Mother*. Here, using a technique which recalls the multiple role-switching in *Light Shining in Buckinghamshire*, which Churchill used to portray the chaos of a (potentially) revolutionary moment, the performers break with their character roles from Part One to represent different Romanian citizens caught up in the December upheaval from 'order' to 'unorder'. The performers were instructed for this section to play their parts in the manner of Romanians speaking with English accents. This technique gave 'a startlingly vivid sense of real events being recalled in the immediate aftermath'.[29] In contrast to Part One, where language has lost its performative function, in Part Two, the revolution is performed through speaking. This was underlined by keeping the performers physically still on stage, posed 'as if for a group photograph', rather than using the revolutionary section of the play as 'an obvious chance for characters to rush around the stage waving flags with holes cut out of them'.[30]

A surreal scene between a vampire and a dog opens the third part, imaging Romania as the poor, starving, ownerless, dog, missing the hated master and looking to the Vampire as a new blood-sucking owner. As the revolution releases the Romanian citizens into speech, confusion and tensions begin to surface. Parents and children are divided over support of new political parties, specifically over whether to be pro- or anti-Front, and racism towards the Hungarians is a source of heated familial debate. Where Lucia created tension in Part One through her marriage to an American, she causes upset in Part Three through the renewal of her relationship with a Hungarian lover. New political 'freedoms' bring new oppressions as citizens like Flavia, who kept their jobs under the old regime, now find their positions at risk. In the hospital where Gabriel Vladu, treated as a wounded hero of the revolution, recuperates, a disorientated patient, representative of post-revolution confusion, wanders the wards asking what had really happened: 'Did we have a revolution or a putsch?' (MF 50) – a line which was greeted with applause when the play was performed in Bucharest.[31]

The re-enactment of the revolution is a theatrical device which Churchill uses in Part Three to dramatize the questions and uncertainties which the Romanians need to express. The wedding couple, Florina and Radu, role-play the execution of the Ceausescus, a sequence which releases hatred, sexism and racism (MF 68–71). The wedding, which Flavia compares to the revolution where 'everyone laughs and cries' and goes 'back behind their masks' (MF 74), re-enacts the before, during and after moments of the revolution, as the polite, public 'masks' are shattered by outbreaks of verbal and physical violence, followed by a silent dance – a ritualized moment of enforced social harmony, which gives way to a renewed linguistic outbreak (in Romanian) of political and social discontents. Churchill uses the high-energy technique of overlapping voices, as she did in Serious Money, to demonstrate the passionate and violent release into 'freedom' which the revolution brings. She assigns the final lines of Mad Forest to the figure of the blood-sucking Vampire who haunts the wedding dance, and instructs that his last few words should be heard alone: 'You begin to want blood. Your limbs ache, your head burns, you have to keep moving faster and faster' (MF 87).

Post-revolutionary 'freedom' offers new possibilities, but like the post-murder release of pain and suffering in Fen, or the post-election chorus of 'five fucking morious' years of Tory corruption in Serious Money, the future for the Romanian people, trying to find their way through the 'Mad (political) Forest' is also 'frightening'.

5

Exploding Words
and Worlds

'Playwrights don't give answers, they ask questions', wrote Churchill in an early essay on theatre.[1] She continued: 'We need to find new questions, which may help us answer the old ones or make them unimportant, and this means new subjects and new form'.[2] The kinds of questions which Churchill asks through her theatre reflect her feminist and socialist viewpoints, but allied to her interrogative, political mode of writing is her experimental approach to dramatic and theatrical form. Churchill's theatre is not just a question of politics, but a politics of style.

This chapter seeks to highlight Churchill's experimental approach to theatre-making by examining her interest in the defamiliarization of our twentieth-century fictions or systems of illusion-making, which she encodes thematically (subject) and stylistically (form) in a range of plays. In particular, it examines Churchill's deformation or explosion of the word, of language, the sign-system through which we mediate and make sense of the world, whether this is in the context of postmodern culture, as in her late 1980s play *Icecream*, or the mythological under-world of one of her more recent, iconoclastic productions, *The Skriker* (1994).

By way of introduction, I wish to return briefly to an earlier period of Churchill's work: specifically to *Traps*, written in 1976 along with *Vinegar Tom* and *Light Shining in Buckinghamshire*, which shows Churchill's early preoccupation with manipulating sign-systems; with 'unfixing' the boundaries of illusion and reality. In the uncertain, unstable, and violent dramatic world of *Traps*, Churchill violates the illusion- and reality-making rules to create a 'reality' that has no existence other than on the stage, like 'an impossible object, or a painting by Escher, where the objects can exist like that on paper, but would be impossible in life' (P1 71). The dramatic world of *Traps* operates through sign-systems which are constantly destabilized: a group of six characters gather in a room which is urbanly and then rurally located; a door which opens for one character appears locked for another; clothes which we see being ironed are re-presented in a crumpled state for ironing; a bowl and plant, which get broken and destroyed, reappear as new; a woman with a baby speaks of not having a baby, and a man talked about as dead walks into the room alive. The dramatic universe is like a Mobius strip, 'the loop [which] has only one surface' (P1 71). In a world in which 'it would be nice to have a family' (P1 92), where it would be possible to 'walk down a normal street . . . or eat dinner in a normal restaurant' (P1 79), nothing is 'normal'. Everything is made strange.

As an ideological and formal experiment with the artifice of the 'real', Churchill baffled critics, who complained that the play's 'purpose . . . remains obscure'.[3] Those like Irving Wardle, who insisted on trying to describe the drama in traditional terms of what happens and who is who, eventually had to admit (disgruntled) defeat.[4] In challenging the ways in which we make sense of meaning, Churchill's experimental style demanded a different 'reading' of the staged world: one where rules are broken and meaning is constantly being made and unmade through the language of performance rather than the word of the dramatic script. This is a characteristic of all the plays discussed in this chapter, beginning with Churchill's 1986 production, *A Mouthful of Birds*.

'UNDEFENDED DAYS': *A MOUTHFUL OF BIRDS*

'I wanted to get away from words', was an explanation which Churchill offered to one reviewer for her production of *A Mouthful of Birds*, co-written with David Lan.[5] In order 'to get away from words' Churchill extended the processes of collaboration to include not just a co-writer, but also a choreographer, namely Ian Spink, director of Second Stride dance company. Churchill had hoped that Spink would work with her on *Fen*, but this had not been possible (*LGP* viii). She had the opportunity to be involved as a writer in a collaborative performance art piece after *Fen*, *Midday Sun* (1984),[6] but was not able to work with Spink until the 1986 production. Where Churchill and Lan shared in the writing process, Spink and Les Waters (director of *Fen*) shared the direction. The play was again workshopped by members of the Joint Stock company, although, unusually in this instance, the group worked intensively and continuously for a twelve-week period without the customary 'writing gap'.[7]

A Mouthful of Birds is fashioned out of seven stories of possession which take their cue from Euripides's *The Bacchae*. As Churchill explains, they did not set out to 'do a version of *The Bacchae* but to look at the same issues of possession, violence and ecstasy' (*MB* 5). The play opens with snapshots from the lives of seven characters: Lena a mother, Marcia a switchboard operator, Derek an unemployed person, Yvonne an acupuncturist, Paul a businessman, Dan a vicar, and Doreen a secretary. The seven characters then excuse themselves from their everyday habits, routines, and commitments and give themselves up to 'an "undefended day" in which there is nothing to protect you from the forces inside and outside yourself' (*MB* 5). Each character goes through her or his own extreme possession sequence. These sequences make up the second, middle part of the play. In a final, third part each character talks, monologue style, about the changes in their lives as a consequence of experiencing possession. As one character summarizes, living through the extremes, experiencing the pleasure of violence, is the 'power' she 'like[s] best in the world. The struggle is every day not to use it' (*MB* 70). Or, as Churchill herself explained,

> For a lot of people, as well as it [violence] being horrible, there is a sort of pleasure in things being so terrible and so extreme. You have to recognise it, otherwise you're only trying to resist it on a rational level which just says this is bad and we don't want it. Actually it's not as simple as that. It's a thing of using your strength and power.[8]

Where Lan's anthropological interest in possession connected to his research of the 'spirit world' in Zimbabwe, used to fight against the oppression of the Smith regime,[9] one of Churchill's 'starting points' was her interest in women and violence (*MB* 5). She was attracted to the demythologization of gender stereotyping which encodes women as peaceful, men as violent. At the start of the play, the women tend to conform to traditional stereotypes; they occupy servicing roles, administering to the needs of others. In possession sequences, however, women demonstrate a capacity for violence which violates 'naturalized' images of femininity. The mother, Lena, for example, is possessed by a spirit who urges her to commit infanticide. A breakfast-time scenario is acted out on four successive days during which Lena is subjected to the split voices of her husband chattering about inconsequentialities (a role stereotypically assigned to women), and of the spirit ordering her to kill the baby. The consequence of this dual logocentric attack on Lena is the killing of the baby, imaged in the washing of a shawl in a baby bath (*MB* 27). Lena states quite simply 'it wasn't me that did it' (*MB* 28).

The secretary Doreen's possession sequence, 'Hot Summer', images another taboo: women being violent with women. The sequence, which begins with a woman-centred text – Doreen speaks of her aching body while it is massaged by another woman – changes register as a woman called Lil verbalizes narratives of violence from a newspaper, to a score of domestic sounds created as Doreen and another woman, Mrs Blair, 'wound' (drown) each other in sound: turning up radios, banging saucepans, knocking over chairs and smashing cutlery. This climaxes in a ritualization of physical violence: Doreen slashes Mrs Blair's face, rolls her body up in a carpet, rolls her out, and the scene resumes quietly, still punctuated by the reading of narratives of violence. Like Lena, Doreen has a one-line explanation, 'all I wanted was peace and quiet' (*MB* 58), delivered directly to the audience at the start of the sequence.

In both of these possession sequences women are aurally assaulted, which initiates a violent release of energy in which they are seen to harm themselves, each other, and, in Lena's case, a daughter. In the final part of Doreen's sequence, she and other women turn their energies from the inward movement of hurting themselves (imaged, for example, in Doreen biting her arm), to an outwards movement, concentrating them into the power to move objects which they send *flying across the room*

(*MB* 66). In the bounded world of the 'rational', women are not able to experience the power of flight.[10] In 'carry[ing]' on her role as secretary, which Doreen describes at the end of the play, she has to repress the memory of violence and of flying; extreme experiences collapsed in the imaging of a 'mouth . . . full of birds which I crunch between my teeth. Their feathers, their blood and broken bones are choking me' (*MB* 71).[11]

The other woman-centred possession sequences are that of Marcia, who as a black medium is colonized by a white spirit, and Yvonne, who struggles with an altogether different spirit in the shape of alcohol. However, critiquing gender stereotypes is not restricted to femininity, but also extends to masculinity. Paul's business discourse – the successful capitalist trading in meat – is displaced in his sequence by a discourse marked by the romantic (traditionally assigned to women), as he falls in love with a pig. Dan, the vicar, announces to the audience at the start of his sequence: 'I don't believe god is necessarily male' (*MB* 37). As he dances, his female and male 'victims' die of pleasure. The dance register encoding androgyny, death and ecstasy is played out against a dialogue shared between a male and female prison officer who attempt, linguistically, to 'fix' the ambiguously gendered body of a multiple murderer.

The 'unfixing' of gendered bodies is most clearly marked in Derek's story, which occupies a central position in the play, opening the second act. In the first act, Derek is introduced as a man who compensates for the emasculation of unemployment through weight training, which marks the body in the sphere of the masculine. He states that he will not be like his father who 'thought he wasn't a man without a job' and 'died within six weeks' (*MB* 20). However, in his possession sequence, played in the presence of Dionysos, he is 'seduced' by the figure of Herculine Barbin. Herculine Barbin/e was a nineteenth-century hermaphrodite who began life as a 'woman', was brought up in a convent, was later redefined as a 'man', and, as a result, committed suicide. Foucault's introduction to the diary memoirs *Herculine Barbin* opens with the question, 'Do we *truly* need a *true* sex?'[12] As Foucault's introduction makes clear, it is the insistence of Western society on a 'true sex' which has gendered the body 'in an order of things where one might have imagined that all that counted was the reality of the body and the intensity of its pleasures'.[13] Derek's possession sequence questions the binary ordering of gender, as Herculine Barbin, played by a woman dressed as a man, verbalizes her/his narrative, while passing *objects from her past'* to Derek (*MB* 51). Her/his narrative is repeated by Derek who *'holds all the objects and has dressed himself in the shawl and petticoat'* (*MB* 52). As Derek repeats the Herculine narrative, Herculine *'stands beside him and takes the objects from him and packs them into her suitcase'* (*MB* 52). As the final signs of femininity are taken away (shawl and petticoat), Derek repeats the loss of the feminine self: 'Sara's body, my girl's body, all lost' (*MB* 54). Appealing to Herculine, who has the 'feminine' packed away in her/his suitcase, he asks 'couldn't you have stayed?', whereupon she/he *'turns back and kisses him on the neck'* (*MB* 54) – indexing the pleasure of the 'unfixed' hermaphroditic body not as two sexes in one, but two bodies as one sex.

In the re-imaging of the murder from *The Bacchae*, which brings the middle possession sequences of the play to a close, it is Derek who, possessed by Pentheus, is dressed as a woman and is torn to pieces by the women. His final monologue, entitled 'body', speaks of his desire for the feminine. Like Schreber, Derek takes pleasure in the corporeal experience of the feminine and he describes the pleasure in his breasts and his waist which 'isn't small but it makes me smile' (*MB* 71). He has 'almost forgotten the man who possessed this body'. The fixed, gendered body of the masculine, a 'skin [which] used to wrap me up', is now open and in flux – 'it lets the world in' (*MB* 71).

Using the body to explore extremes of violence, passion and ecstasy is also a means of exploding the 'word' which binds us to the symbolic 'order of things' in the world of the rational. Spink's movement-based performance register was, therefore, central to the enactment of the 'undefended days'. The dance register was used to create visual, physical texts between scenes, to punctuate or counterpoint verbal sequences, and to encode the classical Greek text in the modern 'world'. As a performance register it was used to signify the relationship between the performer and character and her or his body: 'When the victims dance it is a jerky, autistic ballet of imprisonment. Only when the two figures of Dionysus...take the stage does it expand into the flowing line of those who are at peace with their own bodies'.[14] Working with a physical register enabled transgressive movement between pain and pleasure, terror and ecstasy, life and death, as, for example, in the Fruit Ballet where performers imaged *'the sensuous pleasures of eating and the terrors of being torn up'* (*MB* 28), in Dan's dancing to his victims who died of pleasure, and in the death of Pentheus which used dance to recreate moments of extreme violence and happiness from the play.

As was the case with *Traps*, it is doubtful whether from an audience's and critic's point of view the 'purpose' of *A Mouthful of Birds* was entirely clear. Critics commented repeatedly on spectators walking out before the interval, or, as one reviewer stated, sitting 'it out to the end possessed by a tedium as painfully intense as anything which was happening on stage'.[15] Reviewer Nicholas de Jongh argued that 'this extravaganza of dreamy work, mime and dance does have a clear line of argument and exposition' which was, however, 'easily missed if you do not first read the text'.[16] This suggests that 'getting away from words' posed a difficulty for the British playgoer, educated in a tradition of text-based theatre, but unable to 'read' the physical language of the stage out of which *A Mouthful of Birds* takes its shape.

IDENTITY, CULTURE AND THE POSTMODERN: *ICECREAM*

Churchill's 1989 play *Icecream* also relies on an ability to 'read' the visual, but in a very different way to *A Mouthful of Birds*. For this drama, Churchill returned to working on her own after the workshopping experience of *Serious Money*, which began as *Mouthful of Birds* opened, and further collaboration with Spink in *Fugue*, a dance-drama broadcast on Channel 4 television in 1988.

Like *Traps*, *Icecream* is an exploration and exposition of illusion- and reality-making,[17] but drawing on a more complex and developed counterpointing of visual and verbal 'texts'. There are two acts which are set in Britain and America respectively. As the play opens, an American couple, Lance and Vera, are seen holidaying in Britain. The way in which they 'see' Britain is, however, through tourist images and sign-systems of popular culture. In approaching the Highlands, for example, Lance and Vera sing snatches of half-remembered Scottish ballads, and a refrain from the movie *Brigadoon*. They 'locate' British heritage and culture in a castle setting and a traditional Devon cottage.

By contrast, the quest for heritage takes the American couple out of clichéd tourist locations as they trace Lance's family history to a flat in East London where they find their distant English cousins, Phil and Jaq. This transatlantic encounter occasions a cross-cultural exchange of (mis)-perceived Englishness and Americanicity. If the Americans characterize England as 'the green fields. The accents. The Pubs' (*IC* 11), then the English see America as 'Old Cadillacs. Cactus. Long straight roads' (*IC* 9). Although all four characters speak English, an 'international language' (*IC* 41), it is difference and lack of cultural commonality which emerge, shown, for example, in the different meanings which the same word has in each culture, or how a word like 'icecream' is pronounced differently by English and American speakers.[18]

Loathing for 'American filth' also creeps into Phil's discourse (*IC* 9); a linguistic marker which signals a more sinister note and change in dramatic register. An illicit kiss between Phil and Vera prefigures a violent event, as Phil presents the others with the body of a man he has murdered. As Lance and Vera are drawn into helping dispose of the body in Epping Forest, their English breakfasts no longer delight them, and the idyllic English countryside now represents terror rather than pleasure.

In Act Two, Lance and Vera have returned to America having lent the remainder of their holiday money to Phil, who is convinced that his cousins, like all Americans, have 'plenty of money' (*IC* 24). They are then surprised by Jaq and Phil turning up at their home in America. It is now the turn of the English cousins to play the tourist game as they want to see all the famous sights: 'New York and New Orleans...the Rocky Mountains...the Everglades...the Grand Canyon...Disneyland and Hollywood' (*IC* 32). Again, events take an unexpected turn as Phil is hit by a car (apparently he may have stepped out into the road looking the wrong way),[19] and is killed. Jaq takes to the American roads in Lance and Vera's car on a journey which culminates in a second murder when she (*Thelma and Louise* style) kills an American professor who attempts to assault her. Returning to Lance and Vera, Jaq begs the money for a ticket to

England, although the final scene at the airport shows her tempted to change her 'destination' and to accompany a South American woman on her flight home.

Taking a descriptive line on *Icecream*, as he did with *Traps*, Irving Wardle confessed to not understanding the play 'beyond its assertion that England and America are more dangerous places than tourist brochures suggest'.[20] While *Icecream* is arguably a more obscure piece than some of Churchill's straightforwardly political and/or feminist plays, her interest in what she describes as 'writing more intuitively' in *Icecream* also has a political dimension.[21] As she herself explains, this may not mean 'actually saying "here is a political course of action"', but of 'throwing up worries and questions and complexities which you might not have if you weren't of a particular political complexion'.[22] In *Icecream* the 'worries and questions and complexities' which the play theatricalizes are a reflection on the politics of the postmodern condition, characterized by collapsing cultures, identities, or as Janelle Reinelt and Joseph Roach (via Lyotard) explain, 'the collapse of categories themselves, an implosion that has been attributed to the media-saturated powers of capitalistic production and consumption'.[23] As a 'culture of "hyper-representation"',[24] the postmodern generates anxiety because it is no longer possible to know what is 'real'. In her commentary on advertising in the British media in the late 1980s, Suzanne Moore elaborated on this 'hyper-representation' and question of anxiety, by explaining the postmodern as:

> a time when signs – both visual and linguistic – are no longer monogamous with what they refer to in the 'real' world. They have instead started to copulate madly with each other, producing potential meaning everywhere. In this 'loss of the real', these illegitimate meanings are no longer anchored by the morality of one-to-one representation, float off to produce endless simulations, images of images, fakes of fakes – the past is there to be reinvented because surface reveals not depth, just more surface.[25]

It is this 'loss of the real', the loss of identity and culture in the artifice of the postmodern Western world, which is dramatized in *Icecream*.

Icecream encodes the postmodern interplay of images through its constant referencing of media and cinematic sign-systems, also reflected in Peter Hartwell's cinematographic set designs for the UK and American landscapes. In point of fact, Churchill's feel for the piece, when it first came to her in the mid-1980s, was 'more like an idea for a movie'.[26] Reviewer Michael Billington commented:

> Structurally and thematically I was reminded of the movies: The Man Who Knew Too Much meets Paris, Texas. The first half is exactly like a Hitchcockian movie in which a pair of holidaying Americans turn up in Europe and find themselves in a dizzying whorl of violence. The second half is a truncated road-movie that sees rural America as a disquieting place filled with pockets of eccentricity.[27]

Moreover, Billington argued that Churchill's dramatic organization of quick-changing short scenes required 'the ability of a TV and movie-trained audience to supply missing information for themselves. It is a sharp reminder of how much playwriting is changing in the video age'.[28]

'Loss of the real' is also linguistically encoded in *Icecream*. As language is divorced from reality, it is no longer possible to know what is 'real', what is 'true'. Thinking in clichés provides the only access to cultural identity:

> VERA: When I think of my European ancestors I see this long row of women picking cabbages.
> PHIL: Is that what they did?
> VERA: I've no idea, it's a cliché, I guess I think in clichés all the time. It's depressing but then I think hell, clichés are just what's true, what millions of people have already realised is true.

(IC 13)

Moreover, speaking in clichés initiates dangerous realities. Vera's clichéd 'I would die' for you, addressed to Phil, is immediately followed by Phil's presentation of the murdered body. Death as a cliché, as a figure of speech, is displaced by the figure of a dead body.

Fictions and truths are constantly represented as interchangeable and unstable. When Vera, for example, at the start of Act Two tries to tell her American 'shrink' the truth about the murder in England, he, in turn, translates this into a Freudian fiction or fantasy linked to the anxiety of identity (*IC* 27). Lance's confession of the murder to a colleague turns the truth into a fictitious account of a sexual encounter (*IC* 29), and the murder, narrated as a party-piece to a listening guest at Lance and Vera's party, re-presents the event as a glamorous (movie-style) adventure, to which the guest responds: 'You got away with murder. My god. Some adventure. Wow. Is this true? Jee-zus' (*IC* 35).

The 'loss of the real' is further highlighted in the latter part of Act Two which is thematically marked by the (in)significance of death. Churchill herself noted, 'I didn't realise until I'd finished writing it how much there is about death and ways of facing death, and about things which are buried rather than being faced'.[29] Jaq does not mourn for her brother but embarks on her road movie,[30] during which she encounters a hitchhiker and his mother, who each have their own apocalyptic visions of the millennium, a professor whose wife has recently died a meaningless death of cancer, and, finally, the South American woman passenger at the airport whose grandfather has died. The significance of endings or death is, however, refused as a possibility in the endless, chaotic play of the postmodern. In the 'closure' of *Icecream*, Jaq is still in her movie, is still speaking in clichés: 'I want to be at home and have a cup of tea' (*IC* 51). Continuous (dis)placement is the only 'home' left in our postmodern Western world which refuses to anchor cultures and identities in the 'real'. However, Churchill offers Jaq a way out of this by allowing her to change destinations: 'she goes off to a third world country, to South America'.[31]

'...LIES AND VIDEO TAPE': *HOT FUDGE*

As *Icecream* played for a short, although very intense, seventy-five minutes, Churchill was persuaded by Max Stafford-Clark to introduce a companion piece which would provide the performers who had minor roles in *Icecream* with main parts (*S* intro). Although Churchill had reservations about whether *Hot Fudge*, the play she wrote to go with *Icecream*, would in some way 'spoil' it (*S* intro), stylistically and thematically the two pieces work well together. *Hot Fudge* was given performance readings during May 1989 in the Royal Court Theatre Upstairs.

In a clipped dialogic patterning of scenes, similar to *Icecream*, *Hot Fudge* continues the illusion- and reality-making theme. Echoes of *Serious Money* haunt the opening in which a group of characters explain how to commit fraud through building-society accounts, falsifying claims to money which does not exist. This modern way of 'stealing' is contrasted with a nostalgia for old-fashioned robbery. *Hot Fudge* encodes the postmodern in its commodification of culture, news and geography, as the two central characters, Ruby and Colin, fabricate identities for themselves: Ruby as an owner of a travel agency, Colin as an owner of a media monitoring company. Colin's circle of 1980s Yuppie friends all have careers and lives trading in images. Getting on is not about having the 'real thing' but of having a 'great image' (*S* 293). When confronted by his ex-wife in front of Ruby, Colin's self-created image begins to shatter. Rather than an international trader in news stories, it is revealed that Colin is an unemployed person who has had a breakdown and who spends his days in the bedroom, drinking lager, and videoing the news. As Ruby voluntarily unmasks her fictions, Colin realizes that just about everything he knows about her is also a 'lie', which leaves the couple at the end of the play starting to get to know each other; beginning all over again.

'DANGEROUS LIAISONS': *LIVES OF THE GREAT POISONERS*

After the experience of working alone on *Icecream*, Churchill turned again to shared ways of working with *Mad Forest* in 1990 and, in 1991, *Lives of the Great Poisoners*, which was to prove her most complex collaborative venture to date.

While poison was a thematic starting point (*LGP* ix), experimenting with form in a multidisciplinary context was another. In terms of 'getting away from words', *Poisoners* not only incorporated movement and dance, but also used music in the form of *a cappella* singing. The physical language out of which *Poisoners* takes its shape is reflected in the publication of a production dossier of the performance, rather than a script. The dossier includes dramatic text, directions for dance, the musical score, production photographs (including set design), and images projected in the performance. The different 'languages' of the stage were overseen as follows: Churchill – script; Ian Spink – movement; Orlando Gough – music; and Antony McDonald – design. As the composer, Gough, was interested in exploring the 'physicality of music-making' (*LGP* xi); Spink wanted a dance style 'that could appear out of the action' (*LGP* xv), and McDonald was concerned with 'blurring the line between choreography and design' (*LGP* xvii). Each contribution therefore linked to formal experiment and the desire to work in a performance register which moved away from traditional text-based theatre.

Whereas in *A Mouthful of Birds* it was the case that all performers, irrespective of whether they were trained dancers rather than actors or actresses, or *vice versa*, had to take part in movement-based and dialogue-based sequences, for *Poisoners* it was decided that performers should work exclusively in their specialist disciplines. Only one exception obtained as an actor doubled as a singer. The other eight performers consisted of four dancers, three singers and one actor (*LGP* xvi). This initiated a mode of interdisciplinary dialogic exchange in which, for example, one character might speak in dialogue to another answering in music or dance, and so on.

Poisoners is composed in three sections, each based on the life of a 'great poisoner': Dr Crippen, Medea and Mme de Brinvilliers. In addition, a prologue entitled 'Elixir of Life' theatricalizes a less well known incident from Medea mythology in which Medea uses poison not to kill but to cure, as she administers a revitalizing potion to Jason's ailing father Aeson (*LGP* 5). Like Marlene in *Top Girls*, Midgley, the one twentieth-century character, is able to pass through all scenes, irrespective of dramatic conventions of time. Midgley is based on the early twentieth-century American chemist Thomas Midgley, who was responsible for putting CFCs in fridges and lead in petrol, 'two inventions' which, as Churchill explains, 'seemed a good idea at the time but were inadvertently poisonous' (*LGP* x). Midgley was played by the one performer who crossed disciplines by singing and speaking which, although a practical casting decision (*LGP* viii), underlined his ability to translocate.

Like *Traps*, *Poisoners* creates a 'reality' which can only exist on stage. While McDonald's design needed to set the worlds of Edwardian England, Ancient Greece and seventeenth-century France, it also indexed a trans-historical, trans-mythological world 'outside' of these (*LGP* xvii). As an abstract, three-walled design, it encoded a collapsing of boundaries – spaces which might be closed and open, private and public. As McDonald explains:

> We created interiors and exteriors, both open and private. Performers could appear above the walls or around them and in the gaps or corridors between walls They could be isolated in their own separate worlds and at the same time be overlooked by other performers. (*LGP* xvii–xviii)

In order to link rather than separate the three narratives, McDonald's design exploited the transformability of the theatrical sign. Not only did spaces transform into other spaces, but simple props were used as sign-vehicles to denote a number of different objects: a metal container, introduced in the Crippen sequence, was used first as his wife's jewel box and subsequently became the hat box containing her head. The same container was used again in the other two sections: 'as the vessel that held the poisoned wedding dress given to Creusa and then the casket of letters that contained the evidence that condemned Mme de Brinvilliers' (*LGP* xviii). The costuming of the performers also underlined continuity rather than difference. As McDonald explains, like the set, costumes were not period specific, but were designed 'to create a world of their own', and could be removed through 'the different sections of the story' (*LGP* xviii).

Transformability was also a feature of the distribution of roles. Performers did not so much triple-role-play through each of the three narratives, as transmute between different characters. For example, the female singer who played Crippen's wife Cora appears transformed at the end of the first sequence as Medea, and at the end of the second Medea sequence as Mme Brinvilliers. This initiates complex shifts in agency: the woman who is the poisoned victim (Cora) takes her revenge (Medea) and poisons, and is punished for poisoning (Brinvilliers). Similarly, the actor who played Crippen the poisoner, becomes Jason, victim of Medea's revenge, and in Section Three is Sainte-Croix, Brinvillier's lover. Shifts in agency are underpinned by the dangerous love-triangles which structure each section and initiate violent passions and violent deaths: Crippin poisons Cora because he desires Ethel; Medea poisons Creusa because of her passion for Jason, and Mme Brinvilliers poisons her husband in an attempt to secure her lover, Sainte-Croix (who complicates the third narrative by administering an antidote to Brinvilliers, refusing Mme Brinvilliers, and inadvertently poisoning himself through his own experiments). The triangular shaping of narrative action is echoed in McDonald's three-walled design, the use of three registers (dance, music, acting), and the three lives, three-sectioned structure of *Poisoners*.

That characters were not separate between 'worlds' but encoded traces of their former 'selves' was signed on and through the body in a variety of different ways. For instance, in the second narrative sequence Medea appears to lament over the 'rage' which consumes her: 'I'm the same Medea who cures the sick and brings the dead to life' (*LGP* 34). This was the Medea who was shown in the prologue giving 'life' to Aeson. Later we see Medea transformed into Brinvilliers, administering 'medicine' to the sick which poisons and kills them. The sung lines from the prologue are repeated but inverted: the power to 'heal' through 'hurting' (*LGP* 5) is transformed into the power to 'hurt' through 'healing' (*LGP* 41). It is the 'same' performer who embodies the antithesis to hurt and to heal. It is also the 'same' performer whose head is cut off by her husband in Section One (Cora), and is decapitated on a chopping block (the metal container from Section One) in Section Three (Brinvilliers).

Similarly, vocal and gestural registers are constantly traced across the different sections through the singers and dancers. The gestural imaging of Brinvillier's water torture in Section Three is described as '*reminiscent of Medea pouring potion into Aeson's throat*' (*LGP* 63), and the dancers playing the hospital patients poisoned by Brinvilliers die '*using movements reminiscent of the music hall characters*' (*LGP* 41) which they danced in the Crippen narrative. Cora's music hall song in Section One sings of the Brinvilliers story; the chorus lament for Creusa (*LGP* 37) is echoed in Mme de Sevigne's lyrics on the death of Brinvilliers (*LGP* 65). A game of whist in Crippen's story is used to play out sexual tensions between characters, and in Section Three, in a style reminiscent of Laclos's *Les liaisons dangereuses*, characters play the '*sexy, bitchy and increasingly savage*' game of Hoca (*LGP* 46), and so on. One dominant, repeated motif is the poisoning. The poisonings are not enacted through mimetic representation, but victims are sung and danced to death by a chorus of poisoners. This exemplifies the physicality of the stage language in *Poisoners* – a physicality not reserved just for the dancers, but for the overall concept, design and performance register of the piece.

One might be tempted to argue that the experimental form of *Poisoners* is in itself a sufficient 'purpose' for the piece (although some reviewers argued that this simply did not work),[32] but there are also significant, ideological concerns which unfold in the playing. The 'art' of poisoning is constantly referenced as an 'indetectable' means of administering harm. Like *A Mouthful of Birds*, *Poisoners* makes an 'unseen' or repressed 'truth' visible, demonstrating the dangerous reality of that which we cannot 'see'. *Poisoners* critiques our complicity in the often 'indetectable' ways in which we poison ourselves and our environment, and, importantly, the political fictions which are created to prevent us from seeing the harm we do to ourselves or is done to us.

This is powerfully encoded in Section Three when, in their laboratory, Sainte-Croix, Exili and La Chausee experiment with dangerous poisons in the interests of financial gain – to 'corner the market' (*LGP* 42). A fascinated Midgely watches and speaks of his own discovery of CFCs which he ironically proclaims to be 'non-toxic' (*LGP* 44). As the poisoners continue their experiments, the real danger of their work is exposed in a complex imaging in which M. Brinvilliers is being poisoned by his wife, and Mme Dufay is seen *'powdering herself and clouds of powder rise into the air'* (*LGP* 44). The 'clouds of powder' suggest the mushroom clouds of nuclear poisoning, linking the dangerous experiments to global disaster which affects us all. As Midgley comments, 'something strange is going on here. There's something in the air' (*LGP* 46). The scene continues with a self-poisoning motif as Mme de Sevigne sings of the 'rubbish...we rub on our faces', and Dufay and Sainte-Croix go *'into a face massage dance'* (*LGP* 46). This further links to the self-poisoning signed on the body through the costuming. McDonald explains, for example, how the cast used corsets 'on top of and underneath other garments' to create a 'visual symbol of how we poison ourselves for personal vanity' (*LGP* xviii).

After the death of Mme de Brinvilliers, Sainte-Croix serves coffee and amaretti to the assembled company. When the amaretti are unwrapped, the papers are rolled up, and Sainte-

Croix *'sets fire to them so that the burning paper floats up into the air and the ash floats down'* (*LGP* 65). Like the clouds of dusting powder, this is a powerful (nuclear) image of poisoning the world's atmosphere, underscored by Mme de Sevigne's lyrics which sing of Brinvilliers's poisoned body polluting the air for them all to breathe in. However, the lyrics also reference the body scattered in the air as a form of contagion; poisoning as a disease, a 'mania', which we all breathe in and are infected by.

This links to the political implications of poison as a harmful way of life. The third section uses the seventeenth-century world of immorality, greed and corruption as a means of historicizing the decadence of our own twentieth-century society. In a key speech by Sainte-Croix he states that the harm, the poison, is not just a matter of scandalous love affairs (although in 1990s Britain Tory ministers have given us enough of these), but that 'the whole political life of the country depends on poison' (*LGP* 58). It is a society in which as long as you have 'connections' you do not get punished for poisoning, for harmful acts, and in which everyone in 'public life' simply drinks a daily 'antidote' (*LGP* 58). The political lies go undetected.

In 1990s Britain, we are, perhaps, just beginning to see the unmasking of some of the political fictions which, for example, have denied that drugs issued to soldiers in the Falklands War may have 'poisoned' their bodies and those of their unborn children; that living under overhead power-lines may cause cancer, or, most recently, that BSE can 'poison' humans as well as cattle. As *Poisoners* demonstrates, left undetected, poisonous lies create dangerous, fatal realities.

'A MOUTHFUL OF WORDS': *THE SKRIKER*

Working collaboratively across disciplines tends to confound not only the critics but also the funding bodies, as evidenced during the tour of *Poisoners* when Second Stride found its Arts Council funding cut. As composer Judith Weir, who had previously worked with the company explained, 'Second Stride is a bureaucrat's nightmare no more; the inconvenient mix of dance, theatre, opera and mime, has lost its Arts Council grant'.[33] Not until 1994, therefore, did Churchill have the opportunity to collaborate again with Second Stride when, finally, they were able to work together on *The Skriker* which opened at the Cottesloe, Royal National Theatre, London (January 1994).

In an interview broadcast on the eve of the opening night, Churchill explained how, for the first time, she had sat down to write a play by herself and had ended up writing dance into it in the form of stage directions for dancers.[34] This was, therefore, a different way of working from other collaborative ventures, such as the Joint Stock productions which had had periods of workshopping and research. Churchill further clarified how, during the writing, she had made a decision to pare the central action of the play down to the three main figures – the Skriker and the two young girls, Josie and Lily – and to have the numerous stories and creatures which she had originally thought of weaving into plots and events, enacted in a different way: through dance and music.[35]

The central figure in Churchill's play is the Skriker, described as *'a shapeshifter and death portent, ancient and damaged'* (*TS* 1). As an 'ancient and damaged' figure of a mythological, folkloric, underworld, the Skriker haunts two young girls in the modern world. At the start of the play one girl, Josie, is in a mental institution for having apparently killed her baby daughter; the other, Lily, is pregnant and running away from home. As the Skriker attaches herself to the two girls, shapeshifting through a number of disguises, she tries to lure them both into the underworld of spirits. Josie is transported to the underworld and, after what seems like years there, is brought back to the modern world apparently seconds later. Lily, at the close of the play, leaves her baby in the modern world, believing that, like Josie, she too can be magicked away and back in seconds; but, instead, to her horror, she finds herself trapped in the future, ghastly 'real world' of her granddaughter and great-great-granddaughter.

Both worlds in *The Skriker*, the ancient and the modern, are represented as damaged. Damaged is, arguably, the dominant thematic, linguistic and stylistic register in the play. The underworld of the Skriker is figured as the damaged (Kristevan) semiotic: a marginal word inhabited by misshapen, grotesque, spirit bodies whose 'monumental' configuration of time, space, reality, constantly border, press on the 'real'.[36] In performance, this is visually represented by Spink's silent choreographing of the spirit world among the speaking characters in the modern world, and further imaged in sequences in which business men meet, unaware that they have 'thrumpins' on their shoulders (TS 36), and a family picnic takes place on a beach covered in 'blue men' (TS 48).[37]

The 'real', modern world which the Skriker and the spirits haunt and punctuate is also damaged. Josie and Lily, as the two main characters of the modern world are representative of a non-represented, disempowered class. As young, working-class women their 'future' is as oppressed and 'frightening' as Angie's in Top Girls, or that of the teenage girls in Fen. Moreover, their world is one which echoes the violent landscapes of Icecream or the ecological disasters indexed in Poisoners. It is a world which, as the Skriker describes, is damaged and poisoned by war, drought, Aids, toxic waste (TS 31); in which 'nature' which has always 'been a comfort to people as long as they've existed', is 'not available any more' (TS 43).

If 'mother earth' is no longer life-sustaining, then neither are the mother figures. Josie as a mother, a life-giver, has already become a life-taker before the action begins. Lily, blasted away from her 'rockabye baby gone the treetop' (TS 51) in the closing apocalyptic vision, is left with the howling rage of her daughter's progeny. If the play is 'read', as reviewers variously claimed, as Churchill's way of exploring 'the anxious mood of the nineties'; as 'a chilling look at life at the end of the millennium',[38] then the theme of damaged motherhood may be seen in this context as a specific anxiety of the 1990s; a decade in which the right-wing, reactionary crusade against young, single mothers, like Josie and Lily, remains unabated.[39]

Damaged motherhood and risk to the child (the future) is further represented in The Skriker in a number of different ways. It figures in the fragmented, corrupted lines from nursery rhymes in the Skriker's speech. It is suggested in the narrative fairytale encoding which plays against the traditional, structural motif of the domestic world touched by good magic to bring about a happy-ever-after ending, to show, instead, the mother damaged, not rescued, hurtling towards destructive chaos.

Several of the spirits who haunt the playing space are those who are traditionally thought to prey on young children: RawheadandBloodyBones, 'a nursery goblin who drags children down into marlpits or lurks in dark cupboards'; Jennie Greenteeth, 'a water fairy who drowns children'; Nellie Longarms 'a water spirit who drags children into ponds', and Black Annis who 'devours lambs and young children'.[40] The figure of a dead child sings of the mother who killed her and baked her in a pie to be eaten by her family (TS 19), and the Skriker is particularly concerned to get hold of Lily's baby.

The Skriker's obsession with Lily's baby is an expression of her need. As a figure, the Skriker constitutes a complex, contradictory meshing of transformative powers and a need of others. As Spink explained, 'the Skriker on the one hand seems to have endless powers to transform and to manipulate and to control things, yet at the same time has this desperate need to feed off people', adding that he thought this 'the most interesting character that she [Churchill] has ever written'.[41] To be needed, to be wanted, means that the Skriker must be recognized, be visible, be seen by others, whereas her shapeshifting power resides in invisibility. This duality is imaged in some of the Skriker's shapeshifting which takes the form of very needy figures – an old woman begging for money and affection, a young child needing to be mothered – and her invisible 'appearances'. For example, she becomes part of the sofa which seats Lily and Josie, from where she watches the girls unseen (TS 20), later making herself visible, 'leap[ing]' out of the sofa in the guise of a gaudy, Christmas fairy (TS 22). Her ability to appear and to disappear, her 'active vanishing',[42] gives her power over others; her need to be recognized authorizes power in others. In the 'invisible' spirit world, this is echoed in the silent imaging of the figure of a young girl with a telescope, who gazes on a Green Lady dancing with a Bogle and becomes sad when she can no longer 'see' them. As an unobserved observer of others, of whom she loses sight, the young girl's neediness is physically marked towards the close of the play when she enters with 'bandaged wrists' (TS 49).

The constant play between visibility and invisibility links to the staging of the modern as visible and the mythological as invisible, not as discrete parallels but as interconnecting worlds.

The Skriker, who has known ancient, better times, when people were kinder to spirits and 'used to leave cream in a sorcerer's apprentice', is now damaged, 'poison[ed]' by a hateful and hurtful world (*TS* 4). Similarly, the maternal body is no longer nurtured, protected and cared for in the modern world. As young, single mothers, Josie and Lily are alone in the world. Josie's 'murder' of her young baby is, therefore, an example of how the 'damaged' maternal, in turn harms the child. Connections are further signed through the liminality of the Skriker's body which subverts the binarism of visibility and invisibility, and Lily's pregnant body: the visible, maternal body which carries the invisible child. Lily's experience of pregnancy is mirrored in Josie's experience of the monumental in the underworld, an event, which, as Josie explains to Lily was 'as big as that [pregnancy] is to you' (*TS* 37); and connecting worlds are imaged as Lily's shoe, which she kicks off by the sofa, is reproduced, larger than life, by the spirit world who dance around it (*TS* 41).

Moreover, time, space and reality are uncertain in both worlds. Lured to the underworld, Josie is tempted by the banquet of the spirits, which appears wonderful, but on closer inspection is shown to be '*not working – some of the food is twigs, leaves, beetles, some of the clothes are rags, some of the beautiful people have a claw hand or hideous face*' and the hostess, the Skriker, '*is a fairy queen, dressed grandiosely with lapses*' (*TS* 29). The fantastic feast turns to nightmare as Josie is trapped in the underworld and lives through a lifetime of misery in seconds. Similarly, Lily, in the modern world, is uncertain of what is real, what happens, what is a dream, a nightmare, a state of waking or a state of sleeping (*TS* 22). As in *Icecream*, there is a suggestion that the modern world is constituted by a series of projected images through which we lose touch with the 'real'. Lily, for example, called upon by the Skriker, disguised as an American woman, to explain the workings of television in a hotel bar, delivers a halting narrative of satellites beaming pictures around the world; the television image, a picture, is 'not a solid thing, it's all dots' (*TS* 14).

Lily's halting, broken narrative suggests a further linking of worlds, as her inexpressivity echoes the Skriker's damaged language. After the birth of her baby, for example, traces of the

Skriker's corrupted welcoming-the-baby clichés – 'happy birth to a baby a booby a babbly byebye booboo boohoo hooooo. What a blossom bless'em' (*TS* 36) – are echoed in her speech:

> Everyone says you'll be tired or they…bunnies or fluffy…everything too sweet and you think that's really boring, makes you want to dress her in black but she's not sweet like pink and blue. Or you get them moaning about never get enough sleep or oh my stitches or like that, no one lets on. (*TS* 36)

The play's most striking example of linguistic deformation occurs in the Skriker's long, opening monologue, or as one reviewer described it 'a massive mouthful of words'.[43] For some critics it was Churchill's linguistic play which caught 'the memory', rather than the visual language of performance.[44] While reviewers invariably characterized the Skriker's fragmented, associative speech patterns as 'Joycean', Churchill herself likened the spirit's damaged language to the schizophrenic breakdown of language; language which the Striker is not entirely in control of.[45] Visually, the deformation was also encoded in the Skriker's distorted opening appearance: a 'spidery tangle of arms legs and black wings'.[46] Kathryn Hunter's physical gesturing as the Skriker was as deformed as her language. Her body, limbs, hands, feet, twisted into different spider-like shapes, underscored by the costuming: tufts of greying hair surrounding a face of deathly pallor, limbs banded in black and grey, and a shredded black bodice framed by moth-like wings. At the close of the opening monologue her spirit body, poised with open wings, twisted and turned on the threshold of flight, in conjunction with her linguistic outpouring:

> An open grave must be fed up you go like dust in the sunlight of heart. Gobble gobble says the turkey turnkey key to my heart, gobbledegook de gook is after you. Ready or not here we come quick or dead of night night sleep tightarse. (*TS* 581)

But, like Doreen in *A Mouthful of Birds* whose 'head is filled with horrible images' and whose mouth is choking with the 'feathers…blood…and broken bones' of birds (*MB* 71), the Skriker's body carries the memory of flight in a damaged form. In this respect it is significant that this spirit – 'not a major spirit but a spirit' – (*TS* 16) has a female body: a repressed body,

101

damaged by an ancient past, birthing a catastrophic future.

Although the plays examined in this chapter show Churchill moving away from words into a language of performance, she also stressed at the time of *The Skriker* that she did not see herself 'abandon[ing] words entirely', that she would 'be just as likely to suddenly do a play with a lot of quite complicated text and no dance'.[47] A few months later she demonstrated her dramatic flexibility and on-going commitment to 'words' in her translation of Seneca's tragedy, *Thyestes,* which played at the Royal Court Theatre Upstairs. Her translation of the Roman revenge play resonates with contemporary concerns – as Churchill herself commented, 'the news seems full of revenge stories'.[48] Again, imaged in *Thyestes* is a world being poisoned, where 'river beds are empty' and natural resources are running out, and there is, Churchill explained, no optimistic, 'uplifting' chorus, Greek style. Instead 'the play ends bleakly except for our memory of a chorus who'd hoped for something better'.[49] As in *The Skriker*, the spectator is projected into a world – past, present and future – of global chaos.

The ability to move from the performance-based register of *The Skriker* to the emphasis on the linguistic in *Thyestes* is testimony to Churchill's versatility as a dramatist. Formally, Churchill has demonstrated a remarkable agility, working in a number of different styles, registers and disciplines, just as ideologically and politically she has not become locked into particular 'isms'. 'Her plays', as Judith Mackrell noted during rehearsals for *The Skriker*, 'differ so radically from each other' that 'you can't deduce from them a specific Churchill territory, a specific Churchill stance'.[50] If there is an underlying 'shape' to her theatre and an overall 'message', then perhaps these lie in Churchill's shapeshifting skills and interests; her ability to make visible to the spectator actual and potential dangers of an unequal, *man*made, damaged world, in which women are frequently figured as the most vulnerable and the most at risk.

6

1997 – *Far Away*

'It's unofficial, unannounced and unbelievably overdue, but 1997 is the year of Caryl Churchill', wrote David Benedict in an interview with the playwright in April 1997.[1] 1997 was indeed a landmark year in Churchill's playwriting career, a year which saw major revivals of *Light Shining in Buckinghamshire* and *Cloud Nine*, the staging of three new works: *Hotel*, *This is a Chair*, and *Blue Heart*, and the announcement by Nick Hern of a third collection of plays. At the time when the first edition of this Churchill monograph went into production for publication, it was only possible to include a brief and incomplete postscript on her work in 1997. In the second edition it was possible to offer this fuller picture of Churchill's theatre in 1997 and to include commentary on her first play of the new century: *Far Away*, staged at the close of 2000.

When *Hotel* opened in April 1997, it was Churchill's first new work to be written and performed since *The Skriker* and the translation of *Thyestes* in 1994. Churchill explained in the Benedict interview that the three-year gap was due to having, temporarily at least, given up on writing:

> I just got bored with it. That feeling of 'Was I going to start thinking about another play just because I was a playwright?' I've had it before. I remember that, in 1978, I decided I definitely wasn't going to be a writer any more. It took me about four months to get out of my head the idea that I was a writer and once I'd done it, of course, I started writing again.' ... She looks at me, confidingly, her gaunt gravely beautiful head resting on one hand. 'I think I wanted to wait until I missed it.'[2]

While Churchill took a break from her own writing in the 1990s, studies of her theatre continued to grow, among them a new edited collection of essays,[3] as well as individual essays and articles concerned either with extending critical and theoretical debate on earlier works, or tracing new directions in the Churchill canon.[4]

In her new work from 1997 onwards, one might have expected to find a note of growing optimism, given that this period coincided with the election and rule of a (New) Labour government, the first since Thatcher came to power in 1979. However, despite the change of government, the possibility of a more democratic, less selfish future, remained elusive and Churchill's work has continued to echo the 'frightening' dark note of 1980s plays such as *Top Girls* or *Fen*, or plays from the early to mid-1990s such as *Poisoners* or *The Skriker*. The 1997 revivals of *Light Shining* and *Cloud Nine* captured the mood of a world still very much 'out of joint', while her new plays have variously examined urban alienation (*Hotel*); the alienating dynamic of the familial (*Blue Heart*), and a view of our contemporary world as increasingly de-politicized, inward-looking, self-absorbed: one in which people think only of themselves and fail to act in the interests of others (*This is a Chair*). Failure to connect socially and politically reaches epic, catastrophic proportions in *Far Away*, her first play of the twenty-first century (staged after another three-year break from writing). As this final chapter illustrates, woven through all of these (albeit in different ways) is the thematic of damage: a world put at risk through a politics of greed, self interest, and a social and cultural alienation that keeps us from 'seeing' others (especially those less fortunate than ourselves), and, in consequence, from knowing ourselves.

REVIVALS: *LIGHT SHINING IN BUCKINGHAMSHIRE* AND *CLOUD NINE*

Churchill's revival of *Light Shining* by the Royal National Theatre, under the direction of Mark Wing-Davey, whose work with Churchill most notably includes *Mad Forest* (see Chap. 4), reached the Cottesloe, the National's studio venue, early in 1997 (previously on tour from November 1996). The revival was a critically acclaimed, chilling and timely[5] reminder of missed opportunities; failed revolutionary moments. It was timely not least because the spring tour of 1997 caught the election fever, and the possibility of a New Labour government. While this opened up the glimmer of a more progressive (egalitarian) view of social change, many were quick to point out, even before the May election in which New Labour achieved a landslide victory, the failings of Labour to reform in the interests of a more socially and economically equal society. Paul Foot, son of Labour politician Michael Foot, noted the parallel between the contemporary political scene and the political arguments staged by Churchill in *Light Shining*: in both, politicians did not, despite promises to the contrary, democratize wealth and power: 'Even before New Labour takes office, its leaders are abjectly surrendering economic power to the people who already have it, and, in the process, polluting the political power they seek from the votes of people most of whom have no wealth at all'.[6] Foot's criticism of Tony Blair's soon-to-be leadership, equally could apply to Cromwell and Ireton's betrayal of the people in the Putney Debates at the close of Act One (see Chap. 3, 56).

Moreover, the revival of *Light Shining* chimed with the rising number of homeless people living on the streets, as evidenced on the concrete walkways and underpasses en route to the Royal National Theatre. Inside the theatre, the set for *Light Shining*, austere and practical in design, was evocative of enclosure (metal railings), surveillance (a CCTV camera relayed fragmented images of the performers onto a backcloth) and deprivation (the multi-location, multi-role-playing devices left no one permanently 'owning' their own space; properties were sparse, minimal and functional). The programme notes included a specially commissioned piece by George Monbiot, founder of The Land is Ours campaign,[7] which drew a parallel between the seventeenth-century Diggers who tried to claim land for ordinary people, and modern-day, twentieth-century protesters, fighting against homelessness and capitalist developers who put business before the environment. The publicity poster for the production echoed this: two seventeenth-century costumed figures, one armed with a hand-held shovel, were depicted struggling up-hill against modern, earth-excavating machinery, towering menacingly above them.

In a stark Brechtian montage of scenes, *Light Shining* gave renewed emphasis to Churchill's enduring concern with the (ever-widening gap) between the 'haves' and 'have nots'. This was captured in the image of a golfer juxtaposed with the narration of ordinary people laying claim to land at St George's Hill in Surrey (now a golf course); the new landlord, Star, talking down to the vicar from the height of his 'horse'; and the woman leaving her baby because she is too poor to feed it, her body too under-nourished to provide milk. This last image was particularly vivid. The mother hesitated in front of a stand of lighted candles – the kind you can buy in a church to 'pay' for a prayer. Only she has no money for prayers; no food for her child. A capitalist god does not heed the prayers of the poor. And neither do the propertied classes and politicians – not then, and not now.

If the concrete jungle of the Royal National Theatre as a 'home' for the homeless was encoded in the production of *Light Shining in Buckinghamshire*, then the nineteenth-century architecture of The Old Vic brought a feel of the Empire to Churchill's colonial critique in Act One of *Cloud Nine*, revived in March by the Peter Hall Company as part of its seven-days-a-week repertory season of new and classic plays. I watched this revival from the (giddy) heights of the Baylis circle and, negotiating a view of the stage through the theatre's huge crystal chandelier, I felt as trapped as the family below on their nineteenth-century colonial veranda (complete with stuffed leopard and huge elephant tusks).

Tracks of 1970s popular music (as diverse as Abba and the Sex Pistols) punctuated the playing of Act Two as a reminder of a past decade that had also failed in its revolutionary promise (started in the 1960s) of sexual freedom. The park orgy scene in Act Two seemed as remote as the Ranters at the close of *Light Shining*, clinging to their belief in free love. That attitudes towards sexual politics have regressed rather than progressed since the writing of *Cloud Nine*, was heightened through the figure of Gerry whose sceptre-like haunting of the stage made visible the (more recent) threat of Aids. The performer in this role worked mostly apart from the group and in a different rhythm to the others: a slower, ghost-like movement. Gerry's monologue about having casual sex on a train was moved to the start of Act Two so that Aids and promiscuity overshadowed the opening with the children in the playcentre. The effect of this was to jolt the spectator into an awareness of the homophobic prejudice and panic about gays and Aids in recent years; the ways in which homosexuality has again been viewed, to use Clive's words, as a 'disease more dangerous than diphtheria'.

Benedict Nightingale's review of the Cloud Nine revival pointed to the play's important legacy for questioning gender: 'at least in the theatre, Churchill was the first to ask and answer what are now familiar questions: can the intricacies of sex be summed up in terms such as "straight", "gay", or even "man" and "woman"?'[8] Others were less complimentary, arguing that as a play, Cloud Nine did not accord with the 'classic' status conferred on it by Hall. The idea of a 'classic', however, was one expressed in the very traditional, canonical terms associated with classic realism. Robert Butler, for example, dismissed Cloud Nine as looking 'as if it was devised by a committee', and argued that it could not be deemed a 'classic' because 'at no moment – and this must matter for a classic – do you sense that the characters make the discoveries for themselves'.[9] Churchill provides her own answer to this in the Benedict interview. When Benedict offers the general observation that 'none of her plays follow the traditional route of the journey of a single protagonist' she responds:

> When I was working with Joint Stock, I think there was a strong anti-sentimental feeling about in theatre. There was an attraction to making continuities with dramatic ideas rather than going a long way down an emotional journey...which didn't mean there wouldn't be very emotional things.[10]

Both Light Shining and Cloud Nine need the collective, collaborative ethos for their performances of 'dramatic ideas'.[11] Arguably, what the criticisms of Churchill's proposal for a resistant, post-Brechtian democratization of stage, politics and sexual politics, makes visible is the conservatism of art and of politics at the close of the twentieth century.

URBAN ALIENATION: *HOTEL*

While the revival of Cloud Nine continued to play at the Old Vic, Hotel opened in London. Premiered at the Schauspielhaus in

Hannover on 15 April 1997, *Hotel* transferred to the Place Theatre as part of the 'Spring Loaded' dance festival. The piece renewed Churchill's collaboration with Ian Spink, Orlando Gough and Second Stride. Presented in two parts, *Hotel* was performed by thirteen singers, two dancers and three musicians, under Spink's direction and choreography. Churchill's words for *Hotel* were set to Gough's music. As in the revival of *Light Shining in Buckinghamshire*, the ensemble playing in *Hotel* was quite brilliantly orchestrated and appropriate to an aesthetic of urban alienation and isolation.

The first part, entitled 'Eight Rooms', portrays several different characters spending one night in a hotel. While there are six couples, and two single guests (a business man and a birdbook woman) staying at the hotel, the notional 'eight rooms' required to accommodate all of these characters, are played as one space. The characters treat the hotel room – in which we see a couch, a closet, a sink (with bathroom 'off'), and two beds – as their own, but without interacting with the other couples, or single guests.

The piece is structured out of typical overnight hotel rituals from the moment of arrival and the customary room inspections, through the personal routines of freshening up, changing clothes, getting ready for bed, sleeping badly, and so on, to getting up and choosing a continental or full English breakfast. Finally, there is an instantly recognizable ritual: the business man comes back to pinch the hotel soap.

The simultaneous playing out of these hotel routines among the various guests needs to be seen in order to grasp its effectiveness, and, in particular, to see the potential for comedy. For example, the two beds, key pieces of furniture in a hotel setting, have, at different moments, to accommodate all of the various guests. As Ian Spink states in the programme notes:

> Eight Rooms began as a challenge. How do you fit fourteen hotel guests into one room? What happens when they all eventually go to bed? The potential for enormous traffic jams in such an intimate space seemed huge and fascinating. In rehearsal we were to discover that the simplest of acts, the cleaning of teeth, the hanging up of a dress, the reading of a magazine, demanded a relaxed yet rigorous precision when taking into account the thirteen other occupants of the space. (notes to *H* programme)

Guests take up different sleeping positions on the beds, in various, constantly changing configurations. For example, in the fourth section entitled 'Sleep', the 'silent couple' were framed either side by the 'US couple', who made it seem only 'natural' to be going to bed with two strangers wedged in between them. In addition to the hotel guests, there is also the 'figure' of the television, and a ghost who makes a brief appearance. Both of these roles were played by the same performer. In contrast to the sleepless cacophony of sounds and words which has gone before, the ghost introduces a moment of stillness, quiet, and an emotional plea to come 'into your sleep' .. 'can't you hear / can't you see / it's me (*H* 17). The playing out of intermittent snatches of television programmes and the flicking through channels remind us of how we use the television as background noise to counter the silence of a hotel room, rather than giving it our undivided attention, as we might do under different viewing circumstances at home.

Churchill's text for *Hotel* represents a new departure in her experimental approach to writing for the stage. Where characters might sing or speak to each other in *Lives of the Great Poisoners*, in *Hotel* Churchill's words are entirely sung. The words come in fragments: incomplete sentences, phatic utterances, odd words and sounds. Churchill explains her interest in finding out 'how little...the characters' had to 'say to let us know enough about them', clarifying that she 'decided there would be no complete sentences, just little chunks of what was said or thought, that could be absorbed first time round or in a repeat or even never' (*H*, programme notes). In composing the music, 'a fragmentary libretto', Gough explains that he could 'make the text into music, rather than being dragged along by the words' (*H*, programme notes).

In the second part of *Hotel*, entitled 'Two Nights', the company of singers take on the role of a chorus, singing fragments from a diary found in a hotel room – fragments concerned with bodies disappearing, disappearances and invisibility. The chorus appear and disappear within the set: still the hotel room, but with much of the furniture removed (to make a space for the dancers), and with cracks and apertures in the walls (a 'stripe' in the wallpaper comes out at an angle to create an opening, for instance), for unexplained entrances and exits. The two dancers, one male and one female, each have their own choreographed pieces which seem to connect with the theme of disappearance, but, like the diary fragments, remain unexplained and mysterious. The tone is altogether darker: the music has become oppressive and sinister, and the dancers encode narratives of isolation and desolation, in contrast to the collectively shared ritual of inconsequential hotel routines of the first part. The woman dancer, for example, variously appears in a blood-stained nurse's uniform, white underwear, a black plastic (prostitute's?) outfit, and red evening dress. She handles a small pistol, and is handed (by the chorus) an even bigger gun. While the woman seems to want to lose herself in playing with sinister identities, trying them on and taking them off, the male dancer continues with some of the hotel rituals seen in the first part (an energetic dance routine centred on brushing the teeth, for example), but with hints of suicide narrative. As the piece ends, he is imaged alone, in a state of collapse, possibly dead, by the toilet at the back of the stage.

When reviews of *Hotel* appeared two days after the London opening,[12] they were mostly favourable, with a preference for the first rather than the second part. Judith Mackrell contrasted 'the wonderful vigour of the first half ' to the second which 'ends not with mystery but with a feeling of arbitrariness'.[13] Paul Taylor felt 'you couldn't feel alienating pressure from the surrounding life of the hotel' in the second part,[14] although Benedict Nightingale, puzzling over the 'darker' second section, concluded, 'after a couple of days in some modern hotels, I can share graveyard feelings like those'.[15]

'EIGHT GLIMPSES OF CONTEMPORARY LIFE': *THIS IS A CHAIR*

The 'graveyard feelings' that characterize the second and concluding part to *Hotel* have persisted in Churchill's subsequent writing for the stage. When, two months later, her next, very short piece, *This is a Chair*, was performed by the Court at the Duke of York's (June 1997) under Stephen Daldry's direction,[16] New Labour had won the election. Yet, the change in government came with very little real hope that it would be possible to put right all the wrongs of the last eighteen years, not least because, as *This is a Chair* illustrates, people's lives had become increasingly divorced from the political.

This is a Chair consists of eight scenes that, in the style of Magritte, do not bear any relation to the titles used to announce them. While the titles for each scene suggest major political or social issues on a global scale – 'The Northern Ireland Peace Process' or 'Pornography and Censorship' – each scene, by contrast, offers a glimpse into the private and personal trivia of everyday lives. For example, in the play's opening scene, announced by the title 'The War in Bosnia', a woman arrives in a London street, late for her date who is waiting with a bunch of flowers. She explains to him that she has to cancel, having double-booked herself with a concert arrangement. The characters are not seen again; the cancellation is not significant either in terms of following through relations between the characters, or as an event in a causal chain of action. Churchill, therefore, plays against traditional dramatic conventions that are used to establish character or to set up an action. Instead she offers a moment, an everyday moment in contemporary London, played simply for itself. Other scenes offer interrupted moments of narrative: a mother and father try to get their daughter to eat (a scene which is played twice over at different times); two young men may have caused the death of their sister's boyfriend, whom they accuse of having got her into drugs; a young woman talks to a friend about having a hospital test; two young men (apparently lovers) have a quarrel and are interrupted by a friend, and a couple think they might have heard a bomb going off on their way to bed. Each scene in effect suggests that characters are caught up in much bigger narratives than the audience has access to. Again, Magritte style, each scene contains the possibility of a play that is not a play.

However, the anti-theatrical dramaturgy of *This is a Chair* is also purposeful. As Brecht and the idea of a political theatre are suggested through the use of projected social and political titles, but the political remains absent in the scenes that accompany them, the overall *Gestus* of the play might be argued as the failure of contemporary lives to connect nationally or internationally with the political. The invitation to make a connection between our own lives and the gap between day-to-day lives and the political, was heightened through the staging of

111

the play at the Duke of York's, in which the audience were seated on the stage and the projected titles, performers and fictional 'spaces' were arranged in the auditorium:

> For these eight glimpses of contemporary life, the audience sat in tiered seats on the stage, and the actors performed on a platform spread across the centre stalls. At the end of the eighth play the cast took their seats in the front row of the dress circle while the audience, clapping from the stage (and wondering if we should be bowing), were generously showered with the programmes that had not been available at the start. Back to front you see.[17]

This 'back to front' staging proposed a direct connection between the 'on-stage' lives of the audience and the everyday struggles shown in the scenes – lives, in or out of the theatre, that inhabit a different reality to the global conflict and struggle that surrounds us. This is most clearly illustrated in the last sequence, in which a couple go up to bed wondering if they have heard a bomb. As they talk themselves out of the idea that it might be a bomb, make a note of what time they heard the disturbance, whatever its cause, conversation drifts back to rituals of sleeping and waking:

> MADDY: I'm going to bed.
> ERIC: Go on then, I'm coming.
> MADDY: Yes but do come. You'll sit.
> ERIC: No I am coming.
> MADDY: I'm not sure I'm sleepy anyway.
> ERIC: I'm not going to have a bath I had a bath yesterday I don't feel like a bath.
> MADDY: No don't have a bath have one in the morning.

(TC 31)

As this scene, played to the title 'Genetic Engineering', ends, one final title is projected: 'The Impact of Capitalism on the Former Soviet Union'. In brief, attention momentarily is drawn to a world outside the domestic, but quickly resumes an inward focus on day-to-day living.

Not that this day-to-day living is presented as a comforting or harmonious experience – rather the opposite. People are troubled (as in the 'bomb' sequence), or seen quarrelling (the gay lovers scene). In particular a note of self-destruction or self-pollution resonates through several of the scenes: the daughter who has to be encouraged to eat (rather like the daughter in *Hospital*); the young woman whose hospital test involves a tube down her throat and she debates whether or not to 'poison' her body with drugs to make it easier, or the drug-taking referred to after the two brothers have threatened (and possibly killed) their sister's boyfriend. All of these suggest bodies that are poorly nourished, damaged or even poisoned. Metaphorically, the inward focus might be read as harmful to ourselves; to lives that no longer connect with or are nourished by social and political concerns.

A FAMILY 'REUNION': *BLUE HEART*

In the context of the Churchill canon, the repeat playing of the mother-father-daughter scene in *This is a Chair* is highly significant. The father's role is at once encouraging, then menacing; persuasion is followed by threat. The mother does not object, rather she falls in with her 'supporting' role. The familial and the damage of the familial – particularly to women's lives – has been a continuing concern in Churchill's work, and one that she took as a focus for her next full-length piece, *Blue Heart*, co-produced by Out of Joint and the Royal Court Theatre (premiered at the Theatre Royal Bury St Edmunds, August 1997, before transfer to the Traverse Theatre, Edinburgh, later that month, and to the Royal Court (Duke of York's) in September.)

Like *Hotel*, *Blue Heart* is made up of two separate but related pieces: *Heart's Desire* and *Blue Kettle*. 'They weren't originally destined for the same stage', but as Max Stafford-Clark explains, he and Churchill decided the two short pieces she had 'suited each other well enough to be shown together'.[18] In *Heart's Desire* a family await the return of their daughter who has been away for many years in Australia. In *Blue Kettle* Derek and his girlfriend Enid are caught up in Derek's attempts to make a series of elderly women believe that he is their long-lost son. As in *This is a Chair*, Churchill works theatrically to challenge audience expectations. She undermines, for example, the dramaturgical conventions of a two-act drama where we expect an action to be set up, to be developed, climaxed and concluded across the two acts.

This structuring or de-structuring technique of connected but disconnected parts is emblematic of the defamiliarizing project which is central to *Blue Heart*. If Churchill is, as I maintain, concerned with the demythologization or 'defamiliarization of our twentieth-century fictions or systems of illusion-making' (see Chap. 5, 80), then *Blue Heart* is arguably concerned with the demythologization of the bourgeois family as a twentieth-century fiction.

In many ways, *Heart's Desire* continues an exploration of the motif of family reunion begun in *Icecream*. In *Staging Place* Una Chaudhuri includes discussion of *Icecream* in a chapter devoted to 'America and the limits of homecoming'. In her commentary Chaudhuri explains how '*Icecream* starts where traditional plays often end: with an act of recognition, a family reunion. The [play's] American couple meet their English cousins...as early as the fourth of the play's twenty scenes, in a scene that is a broad parody of the ideas of both family and reunion.'[19] In *Heart's Desire* the entire play is a 'parody' of the family and reunion motif. However, the reunion is not an event out of which actions begin, develop or move forward, nor an act used conventionally to effect closure. Rather it engages in a process of endless deferral as the family members – father, mother, son, and an aunt – keep waiting and waiting for the daughter to come home from Australia. 'She's taking her time' is the father's opening line (*BH* 5), a line which is repeated several times as the waiting-for-the-homecoming scene starts, stops and is re-played many times over, at varying speeds. Not unlike *Traps*, *Heart's Desire* is caught in a loop. The time is the time of *chronos*: 'passing time', as Frank Kermode explains it.[20] It is *chronos* without *kairos*: 'a point in time filled with significance, charged with a meaning derived from its relation to the end',[21] or rather the significant, critical moment of homecoming is endlessly deferred, postponed. It is a time of waiting and also of forgetting; an eternal present in which characters cannot make sense of the moment they are in by referring to a past or projecting forward to a future.

Moreover, as Elin Diamond observes, the 'fairy logic' of *The Skriker*, is back.[22] Although realistically staged in a kitchen – a space symbolic of domestic oppression and in which the monotony of domesticity is suggested through the stylized

way in which the performers routinely set and re-set the table –
the kitchen setting is also a space which is variously invaded by
children (rushing out of a kitchen cupboard); by two gunmen
who burst in and shoot everybody 'dead', by a man who comes
demanding the family's papers, and by a truly wonderful ten-
foot-tall bird. Like Angela Carter's magic realism, Churchill's
'fairy logic' is a means of distorting the 'real', the mimetic, by
the fantastic. In brief, the home, the 'place' of the family is displaced through the citational play which highlights the illusion-
making, representational apparatus of theatre. In *Heart's Desire*
nothing is ever what it seems.

This is equally true of the second play *Blue Kettle* in which
Derek invents and re-invents himself through pretending to be
the son of different mothers. The piece interrogates and
destabilizes notions of identity – most especially in respect of
our sense of identity constructed through familial relations.
Inventions, fabrications and fictions mean that we can no longer
be certain of who we are.

The alienation of the 'real' in *Blue Kettle* is principally enacted
through the corruption of language. Complete sentences are
increasingly broken up as words are replaced by either the word
'blue' or the word 'kettle'. In the final scene, the substitution is
made with only parts of words:

DEREK: What blue me the kettle in the first place was that I met your
son. I did really.

MRS PLANT: My bl? You ket him bl?

DEREK: I was bl Indonesia, his ket was John. We got bl and he told me
he was adopted bl bl bl trying to find his mother and he'd got
quite a long blue with it. BL bl died you see.

(BH 67)

Language, through which we communicate and make sense of
the world, is increasingly damaged, deformed in conjunction
with the intensifying complex play of fictional, familial
identities. As John Peter commented in his review 'the very
language gradually disintegrates; the words become tools of
duplicity and self-defence, conveying meanings they were not
designed to, until they become inarticulate fragments that are
terrifyingly clear'.[23]

Significantly, Derek argues that memory is crucial to identity:
'If you didn't have any [memory] you wouldn't know who you

were would you' (*BH* 56). 'My memories,' states Mrs Vane, one of Derek's 'mothers', 'are definitely what I am' (ibid.). But memory, as *Blue Kettle* illustrates, is not remembering; it is rather a case of misremembering, of forgetting. As in *Hotel*, this second piece of *Blue Heart* strikes a much darker – although arguably more poignant – note than the first. Familial fictions, which play an important part in identity formation, are all the more necessary in later life, the play suggests, to make sense of living in the face of loss, ageing, death. The elderly mothers whom Derek cheats have a need to believe in the fiction of the lost child returned.

In brief, both *Heart's Desire* and *Blue Kettle* deploy a number of dramaturgical strategies to alienate the 'real'; to challenge the tradition of mimesis, thereby inviting us to contemplate a dislocation of family and home; a world in which there is no real sense of belonging. Most significant perhaps is the daughter's absence, continued absence, or non-return in *Heart's Desire*. The daughter, the woman who travels in different countries does not return to the 'place' of home, which is dis-placed, dis-located in the fantastic distortion of the 'real'. As the father states, and repeatedly states: 'She's taking her time'.

FAR AWAY

After this formidable dramatic output in 1997, Churchill took another three-year break from her playwriting, until *Far Away*, her first new piece after *Blue Heart*, played from 30 November to 22 December 2000 in the newly refurbished Royal Court, Sloane Square.[24] Directed by Stephen Daldry (now, as most of the critics pointed out, with the success of his debut film *Billy Elliot* behind him), *Far Away* returned to the ever-widening gap between people's everyday lives and the political that Churchill had dramatized in *This is a Chair*. The failure to connect socially or politically is re-visited with renewed urgency. Darker, bleaker and arguably more 'frightening' than *Chair*, *Far Away* suggests that an absence of social and political responsibility will lead to global catastrophe. Where *This is a Chair* uses a Magritte style of tableau-making to make its point, *Far Away* plays with perspective and illusion to bring into view the 'far away' social and political landscape that people fail to 'see' or overlook. Or rather, *Far Away* insists on seeing differently: that social, not just personal, responsibility for others must come into view if global catastrophe is to be avoided.

For the staging of *Far Away*, the Theatre Upstairs was set with a painted front cloth, reminiscent of earlier popular forms of theatre that emphasized spectacle and the spectacular. Alistair Brotchie's front cloth portrayed an 'idyllic' landscape: water, fields, hills, sky, clouds and an inhabited white cottage (smoke comes out of the chimney). However, given the close proximity of cloth to audience the conventional mode of looking at landscape painting was inverted or reversed: instead of being drawn to a distant horizon, the painting had the claustrophobic effect of being 'in your face'. The blocking of over-bright colours in the landscape (as on the cover of a child's picture book), in conjunction with the spatial arrangement of stage and auditorium, and the very obviously recorded countryside effects of bird noises and running water in Paul Arditti's sound design, worked to suggest the artificial rather than the natural.

In contrast to the landscape of the front cloth, the play opens in a darkened interior. Ian MacNeil's design of the interior, however, shared with Brotchie's front cloth the reversal of perspective. Where *Blue Heart* distorted a realistic kitchen setting through 'fairy logic', MacNeil's design of the sparse interior, surrounded by blackness, brought an epic feel to the domestic. It was rather like looking through a hand-held viewer, but with the image projected through darkness, rather than light. Or, as one reviewer commented, 'the chair and table of the first scene, isolated on a black stage, make you feel as if you're in an old movie'.[25]

In a scene highly reminiscent of the closing moments in *Top Girls* in which Angie, frightened and disturbed by a bad dream, comes down to her 'aunt', *Far Away* begins with an aunt trying to comfort her young niece who has trouble sleeping. The encounter between aunt (Harper) and niece (Joan) is built around the idea of the child who sees more than she should. Exceptionally, and in contrast to much of the adult-child playing in, for example, *Top Girls* or *Fen*, in *Far Away*, Joan was played by a child (Annabelle Seymour-Julen). Churchill depicts Joan not as an innocent, but as insistent on truth-telling – even when the truth means exposing her aunt's home, a place in which she is supposed to be looked after and cared for, as a place in which people, including children, are in danger. Each time Harper believes she has satisfied Joan with her version of events – passing off human screams as the sound of an owl, or blood in the shed as due to the death of a dog – the child counters with something else she has witnessed that throws the adult's explanation into question. When Harper insists that there is no blood, Joan replies by showing her her bare foot, only partially wiped clean of the blood she has stepped in. As Harper (played by Linda Bassett) keeps up her attempts to explain events away, she spits on the raised foot and attempts to wipe it clean. This is not a ritual cleansing, a bathing with clean water to restore, to cleanse the child into innocence. The foot, spat on and roughly rubbed, cannot fully erase the 'dirt' she has seen. Ultimately, however, the child appears willing to be supportive of her aunt's version of events: to be 'part of a big movement now to make things better', and to 'help...clean up in the morning' (FA 14,15). Despite the child's interest in the truth, she acquiesces to adult lies. Alastair Macaulay explained in his review: 'and so a child is taught to accept an appalling view of the world – a paranoid view made up of secrets and lies and escapes and violence on a global scale – in her backyard'.[26]

Part Two shows Joan, several years later, as a young adult working in a hat makers. She and her co-worker Todd are seated at workbenches, each about to start making a hat. The hats they make are not practical, but decorative, and in each of the first four short scenes these hats become more and more outrageous in design and appearance. They are more like fabric sculptures than hats and are talked about as works of art. Todd explains to Joan that he made one hat that 'was an abstract picture of the street, blue for the buses, yellow for the flats, red for the leaves, grey for the sky. Nobody got it but I knew what it was' (FA 16). Their conversation is heavily punctuated by the sounds of the tap, tap, tapping of their hat-making. As reviewer Sam Marlowe described: 'Everything here seems to be sharp; pins stab at felt and flesh, scissors rip through fabric and Paul Arditti's superbly unsettling sound design rends the air with the sounds of tearing and cutting'.[27] The dialogue between Joan and Todd parallels Joan's questioning of her aunt in Part One, as she presses him on the subject of corrupt management – not just of their workplace, but the whole hat industry. While Todd makes noises about challenging the capitalist system in which they are both low-paid workers, any desire for social change is outweighed by his love for Joan, the woman who has 'changed' his life (FA 27).

That Joan and Todd, despite their reservations, participate in an oppressive system, is most powerfully shown in Part Two, Scene Five. In this scene is staged what Churchill's directions describe as: 'a procession of ragged, beaten, chained prisoners, each wearing a hat on their way to execution' (FA 24). In the Court production, the parade-of-prisoners scene was the one scene in the production to make use of the recesses of the playing space. Starting from the back, the procession, consisting of groups of chained prisoners (including children), walked forward and stepped up to be displayed, as if on a catwalk in a beauty pageant. Heads were bowed so that faces were hidden underneath the outrageous hats (including those that Todd and Joan had been making), and the incongruity of the hats was heightened by the way in which they were worn with prison uniforms. This parade of manacled bodies – men, women and children on their way to death, their bodies, along with the hats, to be burnt – was evocative of the twentieth-century holocaust. Todd and Joan do not, however, protest. In the following scene, although they talk about the possibility of corrupt capitalism, they carry on making new hats: their actions 'speak' differently to their words.

In the absence of social responsibility comes chaos and global warfare. Part Three of Far Away is set several years later, back in Harper's house, in a world in which humans and animals are all at war. Joan, the child who first appeared in Harper's house with blood on her feet, is now seen covered, head to toe, in the filth of war. Harper, from an older generation, insists on arguing that it is possible to take sides, to know, for example, that the 'crocodiles are evil and it is always right to be opposed to crocodiles' (FA 32). But Joan and Todd, tired of all the fighting and killing, have 'lost touch' with who to trust, who is in the right, who is in the wrong. In this surreal apocalyptic vision it is not even possible to know, as Joan says, 'whose side the river' is on (FA 38). Joan has apparently deserted her military duties to be with Todd (now her husband) and to have one day away from the killing. But the epic scale of a world at war blows such moments of personal, private intimacy away. The apocalyptic nightmare in *The Skriker*, of a planet destroyed by greed for future generations of children, is no longer 'far away' in the world of fairytales. Rather, it has become a social reality.

As the questions that Joan asked as a child get buried under lies, so other children die, and the world that Joan inherits is one in which it is acceptable for 'children under five' to be killed, and in which people around her are killed by 'heroin, petrol, chainsaws, hairspray, bleach, foxgloves' (*FA* 38). This is a bleak vision for a new century, but one that brings a renewed emphasis to Churchill's concern to show just how 'frightening' the legacy of a world damaged by a political and social creed of self interest is – a legacy that, her theatre tells us, is not so very 'far away'. Rather, despite our unwillingness to look, unless we begin to question and to act in the interests of social change, it is moving ever closer and more clearly into view.

7

A Royal Court Celebration

The principal question you can ask of any artist is: what difference
would it have made if they'd never existed? Would the culture be
poorer? In Caryl's case, the answer is self-evident. (David Hare)[1]

In 2008 Caryl Churchill celebrated her seventieth birthday at the
Royal Court Theatre, the venue she has been most closely
associated with since her professional theatre début in 1972
when *Owners* was staged in the Court's Upstairs studio space. To
celebrate, ten Court writers – including Nicholas Wright who
first directed *Owners* – were each invited to direct a reading of
their favourite Churchill play (see Biographical Outline for full
details). The involvement of the writers in this series of events is
testimony to the exceptional regard in which Churchill is held
by her contemporaries and to the influence of her theatre on
different generations of playwrights.

On the advent of the readings, playwright Mark Ravenhill,
who had chosen to direct *Light Shining in Buckinghamshire*,
summed up the views of many writers, directors and practitioners when he wrote:

> Of all the major forces in British playwriting, I can think of no one
> else who is regarded with such affection and respect by her peers. . .
> it's her ability to continually reinvent the form that most writers
> would identify as her genius. In Churchill's plays, there is a constant
> search for new kinds of language and theatrical structures: devices
> that can reveal the essence of a moment.[2]

As *Far Away* evidences, Churchill's 'language and theatrical
structures' have become increasingly elliptical as she continues
to 'form' political landscapes against the relentless and
destructive tide of capitalism, terror, violence, damaged ecolo-

gies and identities. Dispensing with detailed explanation or contextualization, her recent theatre rapidly discharges the symptoms of a Western world plagued by its failure to be touched by those others, all others, it would sooner impoverish, terrorize, violate, or damage rather than care for.

In their condensed, elliptical, epic styles, each of the three very different plays examined in detail in this chapter share some political stake in reviewing damaging relations to others whether this is the father/child relation in *A Number*, the brokering of power in *Drunk Enough to Say I Love You?* or Israel's relationship to Palestine in *Seven Jewish Children*. Each reveals Churchill's 'genius' for the renewal of theatrical strategies to give emotional weight and political force to the devastation that she reveals at the heart of our contemporary Western world that traffics in a dehumanizing currency of self-serving interests. And as Royal Court productions, each play marks the special relationship she has with the theatre where a new play by Churchill is regarded not just as a performance but as a much anticipated event.

'EMPIRE OF THE SELFSAME': *A NUMBER*

In 2002, thirty years on from her 1972 Royal Court début, Churchill's *A Number* premièred in the Court's Downstairs main house space. Coinciding with the run of *A Number*, the Court also hosted a special series of 'Caryl Churchill Events': rehearsed readings of select early works – *Seagulls*, *Three More Sleepless Nights*, *Moving Clocks Go Slow* and *Owners* – and productions without décor of *This is a Chair*, *Not Not Not Not Not Enough Oxygen* and *Identical Twins*.

Watching back to back performances of *Not...Enough Oxygen* and *Identical Twins* was a particularly powerful reminder for me of how Churchill has always worried at the nightmare world we are creating through ruthless acts of self-preservation which, as *Not...Enough Oxygen* and *Far Away* suggest, bring us to the point of global extinction. These plays also point to Churchill's enduring politicizing strategy of locating the epic, catastrophic effects of violent othering inside the ordinary, everyday details of personal, family lives. *Identical Twins*, for instance, highlights this through its dystopian representation of twin brothers, Clive and Teddy. Performed by actor brothers John and Martin Marquez, the play effected an uncanny staging of the twins as, side by side, they lay in bed narrating the dark and violent secrets of their respective family lives. As children, Clive and Teddy were a dangerous and destructive double; as adults they separate, until a suicidal Clive comes back to Teddy. Guilt-ridden because he stood by and let his wife take her own life when he might have stopped her, Clive kills himself in Teddy's house. Teddy abandons his own wife and children to take on his dead brother's life and family. The nightmare does not end. It goes on:

> Sometimes I think I'll make one effort, not to
> kill myself. I don't want to die. Probably
> Clive meant me to save him. What keeps me awake
> is that I haven't the relief of feeling guilty. (Teddy)[3]

Performed in the Upstairs studio, *Identical Twins* perfected a ghostly double to the Downstairs staging of *A Number*.

A Number has an all-male cast of four characters: Salter and his three sons – Bernard 1 (B1), Bernard 2 (B2) and Michael Black. However, Churchill instructs that the roles are to be played by two actors – one taking the part of Salter; the other playing all three sons (just as Clive and Teddy were originally conceived as parts for one actor).[4] Written in five scenes, the play is continually set *'where Salter lives'* (N 2), and each scene functions as a fragmented part of a 'whole' family drama. In Scene One, Salter is confronted by the younger Bernard (B2) who has discovered he has been cloned, not once but 'a number' of times. At pains to convince B2 that he is 'the one' (N 14), Salter comes up with the story of an older son, killed in a car crash along with the mother and explains his paternal desire to create B2 as a replacement for the loss of his first born. This particular story of origin unravels in the second scene as the first son (B1), estranged from his father, but very much alive, demands to know the truth from Salter about the boys cloned from his body. Switching back to B2 and Salter in Scene Three, it becomes apparent that B1 has caught up with B2, exposing Salter's first explanation of the cloning as a lie. Salter offers B2 another version of events: a wife/mother who committed suicide by throwing herself under a tube train. Frightened by the idea that he might be killed by B1, B2 is now planning to flee the country for good. In Scene Four it is understood that B2 has been killed by B1 and Salter is asking B1 for details of how it happened. The love and loss of one son causes Salter to monologue at length on his abuse of B1 as a child. With the details of exactly how B2 was killed left hanging at the end of Scene Four, Scene Five presents Salter with Michael Black, one of 'a number' of boys cloned at the same time as B2. Michael is the first of the unknown clones to meet with Salter. Unlike the anxieties that B1 and B2 respectively expressed about the cloning, Michael Black is unperturbed, indeed claims he finds it 'delightful' (*N* 48), while a more downbeat Salter is left coming to terms not only with the loss of B2, but also with B1 who has apparently committed suicide. The chance Salter had to be 'back with the first one [son]' (*N* 49) after the death of B2 has been denied him.

Offering this synopsis of *A Number* evidences just how much identity is in flux in the play, particularly if one keeps in mind that the playing of all three sons is by the same performer. In the Court's première of *A Number* the sons were played by Daniel Craig opposite Michael Gambon in the role of Salter. As a spectator at the Royal Court production I found that my viewing of one son was disturbed by the others, and, moreover, was haunted by memories of earlier Churchill productions where performers were doubled in two different roles with resonances occurring between the two. As Dan Rebellato observes, Churchill's doubling has always been done to effect a politicizing, meaning-making purpose: 'When, for example, Carole Hayman played Dull Gret in the first scene of *Top Girls* and then Angie in the later scenes, the first character seemed to hang ghostlike in the presence of the second, and the vision of hell conjured by Gret carried forward and underscored Angie's own journey into nightmare'.[5] *A Number* offers a variation on the doubling convention, however, in so far as it purposefully makes the triple-role playing that much more uncertain in terms of character identity. In practice, the roles of the sons were both differentiated and, to borrow a cloning term, de-differentiated[6] – were, much like Clive and Teddy, ghostly parts of each other invoking the idea of the *doppelganger* death portent. '[D]on't they say you die if you meet yourself?' B2 asks Salter, while apparently maintaining an air of confidence about not being 'frightened to meet any number' of clones (N 9).

Reinforcing the idea of the same and yet not the same body, was the directorial decision taken by Stephen Daldry to avoid external transformations of character (by clothes, hair, make-up, etc.): 'In the end we decided not to do full changes, and found that it would be more powerful to allow the audience to realise that the character has changed in behaviour, rather than notating it through outward choices of costume...'.[7] Craig wore the same T-shirt and jeans for all three of his roles but, playing B2, for instance, spoke in a cockney accent. In brief, this cloning acting technique generally served to embody 'a number' of ideas in the play that question a person's 'uniqueness', or ask whether an individual's identity might be 'damaged' or 'weakened' if it is a part of or belongs to somebody else (N 7).

Given the scientific advances that have been made in new reproductive technologies and human therapeutic cloning, and the leading role Britain has played in this,[8] as much as A Number imagines beyond what is currently and scientifically possible in terms of 'man-made' humans, it nonetheless touches on real contemporary concerns with and anxieties over the kinds of futures that bio-technological advances might be capable of producing. Importantly, however, Churchill puts these concerns to us not as issues, but as 'what if' imaginings located in the embryonic space of a father and son(s) drama.[9] For A Number arguably belongs to a long blood-line of Western family-in-crisis drama, where a crisis is produced by the outing of a well-kept, dark family secret – more specifically bears some family resemblance to theatre such as Ibsen's Ghosts where the wrongs of the father have deadly consequences for the son.

Patriarchally constructed, the role of the father has long been a site of feminist critique in Churchill's work and not least in her 1970s play Cloud Nine. Here, Clive, the patriarch who enshrines the conservative, heterosexual values of family and nation, is figured as the impediment to more radically progressive formations of family and of an acceptance of gay and lesbian identities and relationships (see Chapter 2, 31–7). Similarly, in the moment of 1970s feminist theory, Hélène Cixous, among others, warned of the dangers of 'living under the Empire of the Selfsame'; explained 'history, as a story of phallocentrism', that 'hasn't moved except to repeat itself. "With a difference," as Joyce says. Always the same, with other clothes'.[10] Thirty years on from *Cloud Nine* and Clive has 'fathered' Salter: heir to the 'story of phallocentrism' and, as it turns out, the agent of its (self) destruction. Cloning B1,'scraping cells a speck a speck' (*N* 16), artificially (re)produces a different 'Empire of the Selfsame' – one that vanquishes both paternal and maternal roles. While uncertainty hangs over the truth of what happened to Salter's wife/the mother, nothing is more certain than her absence. But in her absence and in the presence of this techno phase of the 'Selfsame' Salter's paternal identity vanishes too. For this is the 'clone story' as Baudrillard describes it: 'No more mother, no more father: a matrix. And it is the matrix, that of the genetic code, that now infinitely "gives birth" based on a functional mode purged of all aleatory sexuality'.[11] In *A Number* the 'clone story' removes the family from its reproductive, patriarchal history, undoes the '[h]istory of an identity: that of man's becoming recognized by the other (son or woman)'[12] because there is no other to recognize the Law of the Father and keep him in his masterful place. Staring hard at Michael Black in their first encounter Salter observes, 'You don't look at me in the same way'. Black replies, 'I'm looking at someone I don't know of course' (*N* 43). In terms of staging, with nothing more than a wooden floor and a couple of chairs to set the fictional world as *'where Salter lives'*, Daldry's Court production had none of the stage trappings associated with an earlier, twentieth-century tradition of the domestic, family drama. The bareness of the stage, given the removal of the visual signifiers of the domestic home space, signalled an epistemological break with the more familiar terrain of the biologically re-produced and socially sanctioned patriarchal familial set-up.

When the socially constructed roles of family and kinship are posed as being in question then, as the play reveals, patriarchal identity is no longer as secure or certain as it once was. This resonates with contemporary anxieties around masculinity – frequently claimed as being in crisis post feminism's gender quake and in a shifting, post-industrial, socio-economic land-scape where the idea of the male as breadwinner is experienced as a far more vulnerable, uncertain reality. In Salter's case, for example, we are never clear about his professional role, what kind of employment he had, if any. Were they a rich family enquires B1 of Salter – rich enough to afford the cloning? 'I managed. I was spending less', comes the reply (*N* 19). What kind of financial familial support Salter provided is never clarified, though by his own admission he had sufficient means to be in the 'business' of making a family.

What we come to know with more certainty is that Salter made a very bad business of being a father. He was the 'dark dark power' in B1's childhood (*N* 15); the father who neglected, abused and abandoned him as 'this disgusting thing' that 'anyone in their right mind would have squashed' (*N* 40). All of which produced in Salter the desire to make himself a better father by buying himself another chance, another baby. Rather like the cloning process that involves adult cells being able to revert to a de-differentiated state,[13] Salter wanted to reverse his time as a father; to start over again and to manage matters better with B2. Perhaps the bad parenting was not all Salter's fault, B2 speculates. Perhaps it was Salter's genetic make-up, or things that happened to him in his childhood, or may be in a 'different cultural' moment things might have been different, B2 reflects (*N* 33). If nothing else, this is all 'very complicated' (*N* 33) he concludes, while Churchill leaves 'a number' of nature versus nurture questions for her audience to think about.

Nonetheless, in the midst of these 'complicated', unresolved matters, there surfaces a very clear understanding from Churchill that the commoditization, the 'ownership' of life is problematic if not harmful. This is an enduring concern of Churchill's. One can think back, for example, to *Owners* (1972) and Marion's designs on Lisa's baby (see Chapter 2, 22–4), or span the decades of Churchill's work to observe how her plays repeatedly show how capitalist economies of ownership (re)produce damaged futures – *Light Shining, Fen* or *The Skriker*. Whatever else, or whoever else, Salter might be, he is the product of a materialist mind set: sees the clones as 'things' not people (*N* 4) and as an opportunity to make money; to sue on the grounds of damage to B2's 'uniqueness' (*N* 7, even while B2 is in fact a copy of B1). His anger over the discovery of the cloning is triggered by the fact that his own self-serving, designer baby interests have been outsmarted, devalued even, by the production of 'a number' of babies. This was not part of 'the deal'; he wanted 'exclusive' rights (*N* 19). While deftly hinting at the controversial techniques of genetic selection,[14] Churchill prompts us broadly to think about the social, legal and commercial ramifications in our contemporary age when life can be 'cultured up, and enterprised up'.[15]

That Salter has been outsmarted by some enterprising scientist means that in some way, perhaps, he is not wholly to blame for what occurred. As one reviewer suggested, Salter is 'a man who is in the dock, facing the consequences of something that he may not have done, but that nobody else can be accused of'.[16] Equally while patriarchy – especially when one thinks of the corpus of Churchill's plays – is in one sense called to account in *A Number*, it would be wrong to take the view that Churchill is presenting an overly simplistic, one-sided attack on the paternal. Rather, Churchill's portrait of Salter, I would argue, owes something to the representation of a flawed, tragic figure whose actions speak of guilt, self-recrimination and questions of responsibility.

Outmanoeuvred by the gods of scientific enterprise, Salter's hubristic desire for a second chance brings about his own downfall; sets in motion the chain of tragic events in which his nemesis, B1, avenges his lost and abused childhood by killing off the loved son and, by taking his own life, the possibility of any reconciliation with Salter. Discoveries, revelations of identity initiate reversals: B2's contented life with Salter is overturned by the knowledge of B1's existence and love turns to hatred (see *N* 35). As in classical drama, all the dark deeds in *A Number* happen off-stage (we never see the killing of B2 or the suicide of B1) and the on-stage space is reserved for the tidal waves of human emotion that spill over into affective lines of questioning for spectators. True to form, however, Churchill overturns generic expectations of ending in extreme suffering or calamity as she introduces the final scene with Michael Black, the cloned son, unparented, and now happily married and father to three children. He sets a much lighter tone and frustrates Salter's attempts at dialogue beyond the 'trivial like banana icecream nor unifuckingversal like turning over in bed' (*N* 49). Salter's life too is spared, though this comes with the knowledge that carrying on is much harder than if B1 had accepted his offer of suicide. He remains as the melancholic centre of wrongs that have not been righted.

Through Churchill's use of language and form in *A Number* also comes the feeling of a world 'out of joint'. That the 'natural' order of things has been upset is an idea carried through in Churchill's minimalist approach to dialogue where incomplete sentences, little punctuation, are designed to carry the rich emotional fabric of the play. Elliptical exchanges move the characters to points of discovery, understanding and action, but the text is 'ordered' through anarchic trains of thought: 'What I want to know is how you/ actually, what you, how you got him to/ go off to some remote because that's/ what I'm imagining, you don't shoot the/ lodger without the landlady hearing, I/ don't know if you did shoot I don't know/ why I say shoot...' (Salter, imagining B1 killing B2, *N* 38). 'Scraping' language back to 'a speck, a speck', Churchill's textual tissue is a skilful engineering of words; the dissection of words from sentences, strands of meaning-making, that leave audiences to complete the missing DNA.[17]

Similarly, while each scene has a back story point of crisis (the cloning revelation Scene One; B1's arrival Scene Two; B2's reaction to B1 Scene Three; the killing of B2 Scene Four; suicide of B1 Scene Five), 'specks' of information are imparted without detailed explanation or contextualization through conversations joined at some point after the emotional chemistry between Salter and his sons is under way. A question asked or a thought raised in one scene is often not immediately responded to in an exchange, or may be left hanging and returned to in another. B1's interest in knowing whether Salter heard him shouting in the dark when he was a child that he asks about in Scene Two, for example, gets a fuller response from Salter in Scene Four. At this juncture, as Salter offers the details of his abuse of B1 and memories of his son hiding away under the bed (*N* 41), the impact of B1's earlier comment in Scene Two about the recollection of his childhood as being '[a] lot of dust under the bed' (*N* 19) is only then made proper sense of and its import keenly felt. Moreover, Churchill clones topics of conversation in different scenes in ways which, like the sons, make them similar but not the same: the thought that B2 has about how scientists might test the cloned subjects by asking about whether they have asthma or what they might call their dog (see *N* 8), for instance, slips back into different conversations between Salter, B1 and Black. In short, not only does the spectator have to pay close visual attention to which of the sons is in view, but also has to be a very careful listener.

Churchill commands and demands our attention through the way in which time twists from the awful discoveries of the present that drive *A Number* through to its tragic (in terms of B1 and B2) and happier (for Black) conclusions, back to the recovered memories of B1's abused past. Salter's memory is faulty – recollections of a bad story book about an elephant but uncertainty over which of his sons he read it to (*N* 32); two years of abusive behaviour towards B1 that for him collapsed into 'one long night out' (*N* 41). As Salter's victim, B1's memory is of an indefinite time calculated by shouting 'again and again and again, every night' (*N* 24) for the father who never came. In the reunion scene between Salter and B1, B1 experiments with the word 'daddy' (*N* 21); repeats the word four times, a childlike act of naming and greeting the paternal that for B1 is devoid of the affectionate filial belonging the word might, under normal circumstances, signify. Rather, the 'silence' which comes between B1's observation about how 'a dog can become a tyrant to you', and his repetition of 'daddy' refers the paternal signifier back to 'dog' and 'tyrant'. B1 can only relate to Salter/father as an object of hate, an emotion that in turn works affectively on B2 to move him towards a lack of love for the father he was once content with: B2 – 'We both hate you.... Except what he [B1] feels as hate and what/ I feel as hate are completely different/ because what you did to him and what/ you did to me are different things' (*N* 35).

Our treatment of children: how we care for them, what we do to them, what values we pass on to them, what future we create through them has been and continues to be of paramount importance to Churchill (see later in *Seven Jewish Children*). *A Number* represents an ironic twist in the long-standing dramatic tale of the family in crisis as the business of science – rather than feminism – is represented as responsible for unsettling the patriarchal set-up that as *Cloud Nine* and many of Churchill's other plays demonstrate is responsible for damaged children/ futures. The play gives us the moment of patriarchal anagnorisis: the moment when the Emperor finally realizes he has no new clothes, no clothes at all. In the closing moments, the future rests with the contented and parentless clone who muses on a sense of genetic belonging to all others and not just to the human species:

> We've got ninety-nine per cent the same
> genes as any other person. We've got
> ninety per cent the same as a chimpanzee.
> We've got thirty percent the same as a
> lettuce. Does that cheer you up at all?
> I love about the lettuce. It makes me feel
> I belong.

(Michael Black, N 50)

IN BETWEEN TIMES

Churchill's 'genius' for innovation and reinvention makes her a much sought after collaborator, not least by artists whose interdisciplinary practices share her engagement with creating 'new kinds of [performance] language'. Churchill's interdisciplinary collaborations have, therefore, continued alongside her enduring association with the Royal Court. While *A Number* enjoyed huge success at the Court, followed by several national and international revivals and a filming of the play by HBO and the BBC (directed by James Macdonald), Churchill wrote a short monologue, 'She Bit Her Tongue', for the Siobhan Davies Dance Company's *Plants and Ghosts*, performed in the disused USAF Air Force Base, Upper Heyford, Oxfordshire (September 2002). Writing for composer Orlando Gough, like Davies, another of Churchill's Second Stride contacts (see Chapter 5 on *Lives of the Great Poisoners* and *Hotel*),[18] Churchill wrote the libretto for Gough's *We Turned on the Light*. Performed at the BBC proms in July 2006, *We Turned on the Light* is a Skriker-like choral and orchestral composition that warns of the dangers of global warming and climate change. In between these two projects, for the first time since the 1994 production of *The Skriker*, Churchill went back to the Royal National Theatre to work with director Katie Mitchell on a version of Strindberg's *A Dream Play* (2005). This was, however, a different project to her earlier kinds of movement-text collaborations with Ian Spink and others, given

131

that Churchill's text was only partially used. A good proportion of it was surrendered in favour of the dream-based devising work of Mitchell's actors.[19] A strange and curious mix of Strindberg, Churchill and Mitchell, the production's dreamscape, arguably more Mitchell's than Churchill's, nonetheless captured something of a Churchillian flavour in its twisted dream world realities of dissolving identities, damaged relationships and thwarted desires.

'THE MAN WHO FELL IN LOVE WITH AMERICA': *DRUNK ENOUGH TO SAY I LOVE YOU?*

Meanwhile the Royal Court was preparing for a fifty-year celebration of playwriting. In 2006, taking the 1956 landmark production of John Osborne's *Look Back in Anger*, the theatre celebrated fifty years of playwriting in a series of fifty, one-off, rehearsed readings of past plays by Court writers. The celebration included a reading of Churchill's *A Number* (March 2006), but not a revival of *Cloud Nine*, originally planned for the spring of 2006. Instead, November 2006 found Churchill back at the Court with her new play *Drunk Enough to Say I Love You?*

Drunk Enough represents a dangerous liaison between two men, one American and one English. In the single edition of the play text published to accompany the Court prèmiere her characters are named as Sam and Jack, which prompted critics to draw immediate parallels with the US (Uncle Sam) and UK (Union Jack) and the 'special relationship' between Bush and Blair. This association was not one that Churchill had intended, as she explained (an unusual step for Churchill who prefers not to comment on her work) in a note accompanying the play when it subsequently appeared in a fourth collection of her work, published as part of her seventieth birthday celebrations: 'Sam was always Sam, as in Uncle, as in political cartoons where he stands for America. The other character didn't have a name while I was writing the play, and when I had to come up with one I thought of Jack as an everyday name – Jack of all trades, Jack the lad. What I didn't think, stupidly, was Union Jack'.[20] Hence, although Sam was meant to stand for America, Churchill wanted her other character to be an ordinary man who risks the romance of falling for the individualist, capitalist American 'dream'. With this in mind, she subsequently renamed Jack as Guy.

For Churchill's political purpose in *Drunk Enough* is not to focus just on the recent controversial war waged on Iraq, mostly by US and UK forces, but to invoke a much longer, twentieth to twenty-first century sweep of American foreign policy, culled from and influenced by her reading of William Blum's *Rogue State* and *Killing Hope*. The play's depiction of American power mongering trades places with the more familiar, regularly occurring Churchillian landscapes of disempowered and disadvantaged communities; turns the spotlight on to the policymakers, the life-takers, the money-makers, as she did with *Serious Money* in 1987. While *Serious Money* ran the risk of pleasuring those whose wheeling and dealing it sought to criticize (see Chapter 4, 74–5), *Drunk Enough* is unambiguous in its condemnation of an American takeover – or rather a world taken over by American values.

As Churchill showed in *Icecream*, American relations can be dangerous things to have, something Jack discovers over the eight short scenes of *Drunk Enough*. Despite mild protestations of still loving his wife and children in the opening scene, these are not enough to prevent Jack from embarking on his love affair with (Uncle) Sam. In Scene Two, winning elections, rigging elections, getting governments into power and overthrowing governments, all depending on the militaristic and materialistic needs of the American superpower, suggest an exhilarating (sexual) power play for Jack:

JACK: so much fun in my life
SAM: being powerful and being on the side of
    good is
JACK: god must have so much fun
SAM: win win win
JACK: love you more than I can

(*DE* 11)

A slightly more pensive Jack in Scene Three, then rallies to the thrill of bombing country after country: Vietnam, Cambodia, Iraq, Korea, Cuba, Somalia. The list of national casualties goes on. The guys break for coffee, but keep the bombing going.

Some countries are targeted with military action more than once, 'again Iraq Iraq again' (*DE* 15). In *A Number*, Michael Black, expressing his personal views on war to Salter, talks of being 'not at all happy when/ people say we're doing a lot of good/ with our bombing', and of warring parties each claiming that right is on their side. Black confesses he is 'never very/ comfortable with that' (*N* 45). In *Drunk Enough* there are no words of dissent over the bombing. Rather it is the sheer exhilaration and conviction about the relentless bombings that voices Churchill's criticism: to be so absolutely right about this is so very wrong.

Missing his family in Scene Four, a low-spirited Jack is less than enthusiastic about Sam's explanation of how much America needs to exploit the markets of other countries in support of its own needs, though he warms to Sam's spin on the double dealing of weapons and drugs, and the profit to be made from the international drugs trade, publicly condemned but unofficially supported. The lovers quarrel as Sam demands a total commitment from Jack. In spite of Jack's reservations, Scene Five shows their relationship reaching new heights as the two of them are passionate about the opportunities of controlling space for chemical and biological warfare. The 'cloud nine' high of this scene is, however, juxtaposed with the next: Sam chastises Jack's failure to do something about the rising tide of terrorist attacks. This sixth scene closes with a reference to 9/11: 'no no no the towers' (Sam, *DE* 32), and Jack's sense that perhaps living with Sam is no longer an option. Alone for the first time in Scene Seven, Sam monologues on torturing prisoners before Jack returns, missing Sam and wanting to be back with him. In the final scene they are together as their conversation turns to ecological matters that Sam persists do not matter, or can be talked, reassured away. A 'frightened' Jack is self destructing; is smoking a cigarette, much to Sam's annoyance, figuring the health risk to the planet and signifying his own lack of well-being and being well. He cannot find it in him to love Sam, but he cannot bring himself to leave him either.

Churchill, as previously explained, wanted the love story of *Drunk Enough* to represent the love of a man for a country, America, explicitly signalled in the title she first thought of for the play: 'The Man Who Fell in Love with America'. 'A lot of people all over the world' she writes, 'have a kind of romance with America or its culture or the idea of it, even if they also increasingly and simultaneously dislike it'.[21] To fall for the wrong person can be the cause of a terrible 'lovesickness', and as the man in love with America, Jack is represented as an incurable love addict. Once infected with the love malady, Jack has periods of remission but ultimately he is not cured of loving (Uncle) Sam. Sam may be bad for him, but he cannot see an alternative, which is where and how Churchill packs her political punch; states the dangers of romance as a weapon of self-destruction, when we insist on choosing that which, deep down, we know may be bad for us.

At the heart of Jack's addiction (and addiction in the play is figured through coffee drinking, drug taking and smoking), resides a fatal attraction to a politics of ruthless individualism; to an American 'Empire of the Selfsame' whose policy is to exploit all others in the economic interests and welfare of its empire, and to destroy all others who represent a threat to its security. Manipulating the unequal power relations that traditionally underpin popular romance stories, and which have long been the source of feminist objection and critical scrutiny, Churchill places Jack in the feminized position of falling for the charms of a more powerful lover. While romance stories ultimately and conservatively often tend to place the heroine out of danger by allowing for the possibility that the 'beast' of a man she has fallen in love with can be transformed, 'tamed', or 'civilised',[22] *Drunk Enough* refuses the idea of a more civilized partnering given that Sam/America's self-serving interests remain unaltered by the union with Jack. Nor does Churchill opt for a resistant, exiting 'heroine' strategy. Instead Jack remains enthralled to and enslaved by his romance with America.

A demanding lover makes Jack the subservient and submissive partner. The unconditional love Sam dictates makes it difficult for Jack to voice uncertainties he might have about his lover's views and actions:

SAM: what is the matter with you?
JACK: pointing out that it's 80% our own
     companies that benefit from
SAM: generosity
JACK: point one percent of our

SAM: billions of dollars for christsake
JACK: just trying to see
SAM: yes and
JACK: Israel seems to get the largest share of
SAM: you want to go home?

(DE 19)

As this brief extract shows, Sam's staccato-like insistence on being right, whatever the wrongs Jack hints at, his refusal to hear any kind of counter-argument makes it impossible for there to be a dialectical processing or progressing of ideas. End stopping each attempt by Jack 'trying to see' another point of view, or trying to offer a different interpretation of the global market, Sam, with the controlling authority of a parent but the petulance of a child, refuses to change gear or direction. Demanding love, getting angry when Jack begins to recoil from his lover, the one emotion Sam does not display is shame. In the absence of national shame for the wrongs done, there is no conversation to be had that might lead to other kinds of acts of healing or reconciliation.

In her feminist analysis of the cultural politics of emotion, Sara Ahmed maps her discussion of love on to the idea of love for a nation. Working on the idea that unrequited love does not necessarily mean abandoning the love object, but rather can result in an intensification of the emotion ('if you do not love me back, I may love you more as the pain of that non-loving is a sign of what it means not to have this love'), Ahmed carries this through to 'national love', where 'the failure of the nation to "give back" the subject's love works to increase the investment in the nation'.[23] It is not the loss of 'national love' that Jack suffers in Drunk Enough; he does not lose Sam's affections. Rather it is the kind of loving their relationship produces that is the cause of his disquiet and disaffection. Jack's dalliance, his inability to walk irrevocably away, is a sign of his 'investment' in the dream that has turned into a nightmare. Staying put signals Jack's hope that there will yet be a return on his 'investment'. In turn, the possibility that Jack might give up on his 'national love' of America encourages Sam to deploy what Ahmed describes as 'defensive narratives': narratives that 'defend the subject against the loss of the object by enacting the injury that would follow if the object was given up'.[24] Not to be Sam's ally would cause 'injury' to America; would lay it open to attack. Hence each hesitation from Jack is robustly countered with the harm that would be done to the nation if he withdrew his love.

It is significant that in structuring her love story Churchill condenses or collapses what Roland Barthes in his structuralist analysis of *A Lover's Discourse* identifies as the 'happy period' after the moment of falling in love, the moment of *ravissement/* ravishment, into the ' "sequel" . . . the long train of sufferings, wounds, anxieties, distresses, resentments, despairs, embarrassments and deceptions . . .'.[25] Moreover, the exhilaration, the ecstasy of their being together, expressed as torturing, bombing, killing, is antithetical to the idea that love creates something beautiful. That is to say that their love has not been 'sublimated in aesthetic creation', in the way that Barthes argues we are generally persuaded it should be (despite the impossibility of '*lodg[ing]*' love in 'writing'), persuaded that is by '[t]wo powerful myths': 'the Socratic myth (loving serves to "engender a host of beautiful discourses") and the romantic myth (I shall produce an immortal work by writing my passion)'.[26] Instead of 'beautiful discourses', loving Sam creates a 'host' of ugly discourses – of hatred, aggression, greed, or violence. Their being together does not 'produce an immortal work' rather the lovers collude in the rewriting of a report that will have fatal, mortal consequences for others (see Scene Eight).

Haunting the power play of intimacy between two men in *Drunk Enough* is, arguably, the ghost of Churchill's final scene in *Top Girls* in which domestic intimacy frames the political quarrelling of the sisters Joyce and Marlene. As Chapter 2 discusses, the differences between the two women are ideological: Joyce opposes Marlene's 'top girl' views. At the end of their quarrelling, Marlene is drunk enough to want to kiss and make up, but Joyce refuses, 'No, pet. Sorry' (*P2* 141). Joyce's working-class socialism ties her to a political belief system that is stronger than kinship, than her love for her sister, and hers is the voice that gives oppositional weight to the claims Marlene makes for bourgeois feminism. Thinking of the male lovers quarrelling in *Drunk Enough* as the book-end to the sisters' quarrel staged some twenty-five or more years earlier, underscores how 'far away' any opposition to the creed of capitalist greed now appears. Enthralled and yet at times disillusioned by

Sam, Jack, unlike Joyce, has no political calling of his own to stand his ground.

Stylistically *Drunk Enough* is indebted to another quarrel scene of Churchill's: a scene she wrote as an experiment 'using just scraps of what is said and racing through a whole evening in five minutes' in order to address the question of just 'how little do we need to hear to understand what's going on?'[27] It was an experiment that became the 'Hong Kong' scene in *This is a Chair* in which two men, seemingly lovers, quarrel, get interrupted by a friend and manage a more amicable note between them before the scene ends (see Chapter 6, 111). What Churchill recollects is how hard it was to work out how to play the scene: 'it took a disproportionate amount of rehearsal: if time passes between every line, should the gestures and position of the actors change? And the scene has to go fast, of course, with no gaps for the missing time'.[28] Resuming the threads of this experiment in the highly elliptical *Drunk Enough* poses director and actors with similar questions about how to perform the scenes which leap-frog over episodes of American foreign policy dating back to the Second World War and converse them into happening in the here and now timeline of the lovers' affair. As director James Macdonald explains '[w]hen real time is shredded as it is in this text it's hard to decide what to show'.[29] Macdonald's decision to focus on the 'love story' rather than attempting 'to show any reality to the political work, which is anyway skipping through time so fast it would be hard to capture', heightened the sense of the lovers' world as dislocated from the 'reality' around them.[30]

Chewing up history and spitting it out in the pain and ecstasy of 'a lover's discourse', *Drunk Enough*, while it bears some family resemblance to the elliptical style of *A Number*, is even more 'shredded', distilled into a barely punctuated volley of words eschewing all extraneous details; minimalist to the point of vanishing. Where *A Number* specifies a location and offers the tip of a family iceberg for the actors to work on, *Drunk Enough* has the complex, international back-story of American foreign policy for the actors to fathom[31] and is devoid of any instructions for the setting. As a solution for setting the play Macdonald came up with the idea of a suspended sofa: 'in mid-air, both domestic and intimate, but also somehow removed from reality'.[32] After each scene came a blackout and a resetting of the sofa, each time raised a little higher so that, watching the performance from the circle of the Court, I eventually found the performers rising almost to my eye level. Edged by rows of dressing-room light bulbs on an otherwise dark and empty stage, the elevated two-man sofa suggested that nobody and nothing outside of the two of them mattered. At once an evocation of the idea that falling in love means falling into a state of oblivion it was also a powerful comment on being oblivious to the voiding of lives destroyed by their dangerous romantic liaison.

Similar to other of Churchill's plays, *Drunk Enough* not so much ends as suspends the spectator in a 'frightening' nightmare. Like Joan in *Far Away*, for instance, Jack has stepped into a current of global violence that, at times, he may have questioned but ultimately has become party to and a part of. In his Beckettian coupling with Sam, Jack is left waiting, 'frightened', 'hopeless', 'dead' (*DE* 41–2); nowhere else to go; no one else he would rather be with.

At the heart of *Drunk Enough* is a romance story that demonstrates a loss of selfhood; of a self that is consumed by taking on and being taken over by the values of the love object. Self consumption was a topic Churchill returned to in her task of translating Olivier Choinière's *Félicité/Bliss*, which opened at the Court in March 2008. A surreal treatment of identity dissolving into celebrity magazine culture, Choinière's dramatization of private lives turned inside out, or outside in, morphing public into private, private into public stories, resonates with Churchill's own preoccupations with the volatility of contemporary constructions of identity.

In September 2008, as the Court staged Churchill's birthday celebration with the rehearsed readings of the ten plays from *Owners* through to *A Number*, it provided a snapshot of her enduring concern with lives consumed by social, cultural and political values that are both self-harming and harmful to others. Her representations of a world increasingly scarred by inhumanity as its inhabitants seek personal happiness, 'bliss', as illustrated in *Far Away* or *Drunk Enough*, suggest an incurable addiction to a global capitalist 'empire of the Selfsame' – an empire founded not on love or amity, but on hate and conflict.

'A PLAY FOR GAZA': *SEVEN JEWISH CHILDREN*

In late December 2008, the on-going conflict in the Middle East between Israel and Palestine escalated. Israel launched a military attack on Gaza and between 27 December 2008 and 18 January 2009 the bombing of the Gaza Strip saw a heavy number of Palestinian casualties, many of whom were civilians; many of whom were children. No stranger to protests and rallies against local and global injustices, and a supporter of the Palestine Solidarity Campaign,[33] Churchill was among the many protestors who joined the march from Hyde Park Corner to the Israeli Embassy in London to call an end to the atrocities in Gaza. During the protest, she found herself marching alongside medics belonging to the organization Medical Aid for Palestinians (MAP) and wanting to be of some 'tactical use' to the organization.[34] Theatre she recognized as a way of bringing people together to support Gaza and as a means of offering practical support by raising money.

Churchill's practical and tactical response, therefore, was to write *Seven Jewish Children* as 'a play for Gaza', made freely available via the web, with performances licensed free of charge conditional upon there being a collection in aid of MAP.[35] She wrote the play quickly during the war on Gaza as a response to what was happening there, and just as quickly the Royal Court agreed to stage it. Prior to the production which opened on 6 February 2009, the *Guardian* arts correspondent Mark Brown reported director Dominic Cooke's claim that one of the Court's 'strengths was its willingness to react to events – but this was the quickest turnaround he had known. "I hope audiences will be moved by the play," he said. "I hope they'll be provoked, that they'll be made to think about the historical circumstances that have led us to the situation in the Middle East"'.[36] That the play 'might be provocative' had clearly crossed Cooke's mind, while director of the Royal Court's International Department, Elyse Dodgson, was also minded to offer an implicitly defensive view of the play: '"...It is not an attack on anyone, it is a cry of grief"'.[37]

The play was, however, received by leaders and defenders of the Jewish community in Britain as an anti-Semitic 'attack' on their communities.[38] From this short, ten-minute play burst an epic volley in the press of what Churchill described, when defending *Seven Jewish Children*, as a pantomime styled series of anti-Semitic accusations and rebuttals – ' "Oh yes you are", "Oh no I'm not" '.[39] Moreover, since the Court's production, the controversy has been reignited on account of the BBC's decision not to broadcast the play on radio on the grounds of 'impartiality';[40] the *Guardian's* web posting of the play performed by Jennie Stoller,[41] and international performances of *Seven Jewish Children*[42] that have sparked the anti-Semitic debate in other countries (especially in the US). From Churchill's point of view, the argument over whether the play is or is not anti-Semitic serves 'to distract attention from Israel'[43] and from her purpose in wanting, through theatre, to offer much needed aid to Palestinians.

In defence of Churchill's play it is important to understand how the writing is driven by the question that the opening scene of *Far Away* stages between Harper and her niece Joan: of what to say to children about the violence of the world they inhabit – 'It's all about families talking about what they will or won't tell their children about what's going on'.[44] This was underscored in the Court's production as in order to accommodate *Seven Jewish Children* into its production schedule, Churchill's play shared the Downstairs stage with Marius von Mayenburg's *The Stone*. Opening the Court's season of new plays about Germany, *The Stone* is a family drama that retells decades of German history between 1935 and 1993 through a generational trio of women – grandmother, mother and daughter. Moving back to a house in Dresden that the family occupied in the past, the women uncover familial fabrications and fictions that disguise the reality of a more shameful past; of a grandfather who may well have colluded in the deaths of a Jewish couple, in contrast to the handed down belief that he helped them to escape the Nazis. 'What are you going to tell your daughter?' the grandfather, drunk during an air raid in 1945 asks his wife, as he refuses the basement of the house as a place of safety from the bombing.[45] The question is rich in ambiguity: how to explain to a child the war, the danger, the need to be in a basement away from the

141

bombs, and, implicitly, what in the future is to be told about lives destroyed by war and the guilt in destroying the lives of others. In brief, the questions raised by Mayenburg's play helped set the scene for Churchill's *Seven Jewish Children* to pick up the historical threads from the Holocaust through to the war in Gaza in a complex familial questioning of what should or should not be said to different generations of Jewish children. As theatre critic Michael Billington observed 'Whereas *The Stone* shows how German children are often the victims of lies about family history, Churchill's play suggests Israeli children are subject to a barrage of contradictory information about past and present'.[46]

After the performance of *The Stone*, the white cube setting for Mayenburg's play was lit in a blue wash of colour and reset with a large family dining table laid with a loaf of bread and a knife. Entering through the auditorium, the all Jewish cast of nine,[47] quite formally costumed (the women predominantly in black dresses; the men in white shirts and dark trousers) took up their positions, some seated at the table, some to the sides, all continually on-stage throughout, whatever the configuration of performers used for each scene.

Domestically set, each scene presents adults in conversation about what they should or should not tell a girl child, whom we never see, about the dangers, threats, or violence that is all around her. Grouped around the table, relatives of the girl intone a series of imperatives:

Tell her it's a game
Tell her it's serious
But don't frighten her
Don't tell her they'll kill her.

(SJC 1)[48]

Between the lines of the opening scene ghosts the Holocaust: the need for the child to be kept hidden, quiet in a place of safety and not to understand the real danger she is in. Each of the play's seven scenes continue in the same poetic style of lament, though each shifts in time from the Holocaust through to the present moment in Gaza, taking in emigration to Israel, the Six-Day War, and the on-going hostilities between Israel and Palestine signified by the building of the wall 'to keep us [Israel] safe' (*SJC* 6). No same child is addressed (given the time shifts) and family members change and rearrange themselves around the table.

As the play, through this domestic scenario, traverses an epic canvas from the Holocaust to the war in Gaza, just as *Drunk Enough* distils decades of American policy into the life span of a love affair, what is striking is its refrain of uncertainty. There is no univocal declaration of what should be said or not said to the child, but a juggling and warring of what to hold back, to conceal, or what to reveal. What to tell the child, for instance, about the land and home that is now 'hers' but has displaced others:

> Tell her to be careful.
> Don't tell her who used to live in this house.
> No, but don't tell her her great great grandfather used to live in this house
> No but don't tell her Arabs used to sleep in her bedroom.
>
> (*SJC* 4)

In the absence of definitive answers what surfaces is the anguish of self-reflexive parental or familial concern for how the nightmare realities of warring hostilities can be translated into something that does not 'frighten' a child. For the spectator this translates into the only desirable solution: a cessation of hostilities.

The final scene of *Seven Jewish Children* is one that has attracted a good deal of criticism from the play's detractors and anti-Semitic accusers. It abandons the single line refrain of 'tell her' for a much longer outburst; a monologue venting, boiling over into the idea of telling the girl what 'the whole world knows'; '...tell/ her there's dead babies, did she see babies? tell her she's got/ nothing to be ashamed of...' (*SJC* 7). (In the Court production the scene was played between a man, woman and an older female relative, with the monologue assigned to the man.) The outburst is hard-hitting: 'the iron fist' of a remorseless Israel refuses to 'stop killing them till we're safe'; '...tell her I look at one of their children covered in/ blood and what do I feel? tell her all I feel is happy it's not her' (*SJC* 7).[49] Seeing one dead Palestinian child among many, what he sees and feels is the relief of knowing his own child is safe, unharmed. The safety of his own kind is the barrier, the wall, that defends him and prevents him from connecting to the loss, the grief of others. Seeing the love for and connection to those who are not our own is, as Churchill has represented throughout her theatre, urgently needed in the interests of less damaging, 'frightening' futures.

When it comes, towards the close of the play, this outburst is indeed shocking but then Churchill argues it needs to be: 'His outburst is meant, in a small way, to shock during a shocking situation. Is it worse than a picture of Israelis dancing for joy as smoke rises over Gaza? Or the text of Rabbi Shloyo Aviner's booklet distributed to soldiers saying cruelty is sometimes a good attribute?'[50] As Black would say in *A Number*, 'I'm never very comfortable with that' (*N* 45). Discomforting her audience is Churchill's tactic for pressing home the point that without a cessation of hostilities it is impossible to utter the imperative 'Tell her she is, and all other children are, safe'.

By Churchill's own admission, *Seven Jewish Children* was conceived as 'a political event not just a theatre event'.[51] That does not, however, mean that her playwriting is simply or merely didactic. Rather her 'genius', as her work past and present at the Royal Court and elsewhere evidences, is her ability to distil the political into shapeshifting Churchillian landscapes that while painful, on occasion almost too painful, to contemplate, urge a consideration of the 'frightening' empires that are of our own, 'Selfsame' making.

Notes

CHAPTER 1. BEGINNINGS: RADIO, STAGE AND TELEVISION

1 Churchill, quoted in Judith Thurman, 'The Playwright Who Makes you Laugh about Orgasm, Racism, Class Struggle, Homophobia, Woman-Hating, the British Empire, and the Irrepressible Strangeness of the Human Heart', *Ms.*, May 1982, 51–7; 54.

2 Geraldine Cousin interview, *New Theatre Quarterly* Vol. IV, no. 13 (February 1988), 3–16; 3.

3 Ibid.

4 Ibid., 4.

5 Thurman, *Ms.*, May 1982, 51, 54.

6 Ibid., 51.

7 See chronology for details of early performed work. For details of early unperformed work, see Linda Fitzsimmons, *File on Churchill* (London: Methuen, 1989), 10–12.

8 Churchill, however, has stated that she was not aware of Freud's study at the time of writing. See Amelia Howe Kritzer, *The Plays of Caryl Churchill: Theatre of Empowerment* (Basingstoke: Macmillan, 1991), 202, n. 17.

9 Hélène Cixous, 'The Laugh of the Medusa', in Elaine Marks and Isabelle de Courtivron (eds), *New French Feminisms* (Brighton: Harvester, 1981), 245–64; 245.

10 Kritzer, 33. *The Female Malady* (London: Virago, 1987) is Elaine Showalter's study of women and madness.

11 Kritzer, 36.

12 Churchill cites chapter 5 of Fanon's *The Wretched of the Earth* (Harmondsworth: Penguin, 1967) as a reference point (*S.* 96).

13 *Black Skins, White Masks* is the title of a later study by Fanon, published in 1967. Churchill states that this 'was one of the things (along with Genet) that led to Joshua, the black servant, being played by a white in *Cloud Nine*' (*S.* Intro).

14 R. D. Laing, *The Divided Self* (1960; Harmondsworth: Penguin/ Pelican, 1965), 181.

15 On the rhetoric of the starving body as guilt, imperialism and war, see Maud Ellmann on Jane Fonda's Keep Fit programme and diet as response to the Vietnam War in *The Hunger Artists* (London: Virago, 1993), 9–11.

16 In *Top Girls* Angie puts on a dress which is now too small for her, but which is significant because it was given to her by her real mother, Marlene, in order, she states, 'to kill my mother' (*P2* 98).

17 Quoted in Fitzsimmons, 18.

18 Jackie Kay interview, *New Statesman and Society*, 21 April 1989, 41–2; 42.

19 See my *An introduction to Feminism and Theatre* (London: Routledge, 1995), 143.

CHAPTER 2. THE 'WOMAN WRITER'

1 Ann McFerran 'The Theatre's (Somewhat) Angry Young Women', *Time Out*, 28 October–3 November 1977, 13–15.

2 Gillian Hanna, introduction to *Monstrous Regiment: A Collective Celebration* (London: Nick Hern, 1991), xxvii–xxix.

3 McFerran, 13.

4 Ibid.

5 Ibid., 15.

6 Churchill in 'Caryl Churchill', in Kathleen Betsko and Rachel Koenig (eds), *Interviews with Contemporary Women Playwrights*, (New York: Beech Tree Books, 1987), 75–84; 76.

7 For plot descriptions of these two unpublished plays, see Geraldine Cousin, *Churchill the Playwright*, (London: Methuen, 1989), 107–9.

8 See Sue-Ellen Case, *Feminism and Theatre* (Basingstoke: Macmillan, 1988), chapter 7, 'Towards a New Poetics', for an overview of developments in feminist theory, film and performance.

9 Churchill in 'Caryl Churchill, author of this month's playtext, talks to p & p', *Plays and Players*, January 1973, 40 and p. 1 of special inset publishing script of *Owners*; 40.

10 Ibid.

11 *Plays and Players*, February 1973, 41–2; 42.

12 Ibid.

13 *Plays and Players*, January 1973, inset p. 1.

14 Hélène Cixous and Catherine Clément. *The Newly Born Woman* (Manchester: Manchester University Press, 1987), 78.

15 Ibid. 80. On the mastery of women by men see also Eva Figes, *Patriarchal Attitudes* (1970; London: Faber and Faber, 1978), which Churchill states she had read not long before the writing of *Owners* and 'which may have affected the character of Clegg' (*P1* 4).

16 Phyllis Chesler, *Sacred Bond: Motherhood Under Siege* (London: Virago, 1990), 122.

17 The Baby M case took place in the mid-1980s when Mary Beth Whitehead agreed to be paid to give birth to a baby for William and Elizabeth Stern. She changed her mind after the birth, which gave rise to a highly publicized court battle in which she, as the birth mother, lost her rights to the child.

18 For further discussion of this point, see Peggy Phelan on 'White men and pregnancy: discovering the body to be rescued', in *Unmarked* (London: Routledge, 1993), 130–45.

19 See, for example, Adrienne Rich, *of Woman Born* (London: Virago, 1977).

20 The Channel 4 documentary *The Dying Rooms*, broadcast in 1995, revealed the appalling conditions of orphanages which house the abandoned girl children of China.

21 The natural resources issue was pressing in the early 1970s, culminating in the oil crisis in 1973, but, arguably, matters of ecology have become even more pressing in recent years with the concern for global warming, the destruction of the rain forests, the continued abuse of other natural resources, and so on. It remains an urgent issue in Churchill's theatre; see, for example discussion of plays in Chapter 5.

22 *New Statesmen and Society*, 21 April 1989, 41.

23 Churchill, quoted in Catherine Itzin, *Stages in the Revolution* (London: Methuen, 1980), 282.

24 Churchill in McFerran's interview, 13.

25 Quoted in Elaine Aston (ed.), *Feminist Theatre Voices: A Collective Oral History* (Loughborough: Loughborough Theatre Texts, 1997), 70.

26 Churchill interview in Betsko and Koenig (eds), 77.

27 David Zane Mairowitz, 'God and the Devil', *Plays and Players*, February 1977, 24–5; 25.

28 Ibid.

29 *Spare Rib*, December 1976, 38.

30 *The Times*, 8 December 1976, 11.

31 Gillian Hanna, *Feminism and Theatre*, Theatre Papers, 2nd series, no. 8 (Dartington, Devon: Dartington College, 1978), 9.

32 Wandor, *Spare Rib*, 1976, 38.

33 Clément, in Cixous and Clément, 8.

34 Ibid., 7.

35 For an overview of Irigaray's speculum, see Toril Moi, *Sexual/Textual Politics: Feminist Literary Theory* (London: Routledge, 1985), 127–31.

36 Hanna, 1978, 9–10.

37 Reported in the *Guardian*, 'Home News' section, 12 October 1993, 2.

38 Michèle Roberts, review of *Floorshow, Spare Rib*, January 1978, 38.
39 Churchill, *Omnibus*, BBC1, November 1988.
40 Sue-Ellen Case and Jeanie K. Forte, 'From Formalism to Feminism', *Theater* 16 (1985), 62–5; 65.
41 Elizabeth Grosz, *Volatile Bodies: Toward a Corporeal Feminism* (Bloomington and Indianapolis: Indiana University Press, 1994), 199.
42 Susan Carlson, 'Comic Collisions: Convention, Rage, and Order', *New Theatre Quarterly*, 12 (November 1987), 303–16; 313.
43 Antony Sher in Rob Ritchie, (ed.), *The Joint Stock Book* (London: Methuen, 1987), 139–40. For further details of the workshopping and rehearsal processes see Michelene Wandor, 'Free Collective Bargaining', in *Time Out*, 30 March–5 April 1979, 14-16.
44 Lynne Truss interview, *Plays and Players*, January 1984, 8–10; 10.
45 John Simon interview, *Vogue*, August 1983, 126 and 130; 126.
46 *Plays and Players*, May 1979, 23.
47 Quoted in Thurman, *Ms.*, May 1982, 54,
48 Lynne Truss interview, *Plays and Players*, January 1984, 8.
49 Ibid.
50 Written in 1979, performed in 1980 at the Soho Poly, and published in *Churchill: Shorts*, 245–73.
51 Elin Diamond, '(In)Visible Bodies in Churchill's Theater', in Lynda Hart (ed.), *Making a Spectacle* (Ann Arbor: University of Michigan Press, 1989), 259–81; 266.
52 *Plays and Players*, November 1982, 22–3; 23.
53 Sue-Ellen Case, *Feminism and Theatre*, 87.
54 Pat Barr's study of Isabella Bird, *A Curious Life for a Lady* (London: Secker & Warburg, 1970), which Churchill used as background research for *Top Girls*, also notes that Hennie (like Joyce), in contrast to Isabella (like Marlene), satisfied a maternal need by looking after and educating a young girl from their village.
55 Joseph Marohl, 'De-realised Women: Performance and Identity in *Top Girls*', *Modern Drama*, vol. 30, no. 3 (September 1987), 376–88; 377.
56 *Plays and Players*, May 1991, 25.
57 See Susan Faludi's *Backlash* (London: Vintage, 1991 and 1992).
58 For details, see Fitzsimmons, *File on Churchill*, 8.
59 Quoted in *Feminist Theatre Voices*, 69.
60 Christopher Innes, *Modern British Drama 1890–1990* (Cambridge: Cambridge University Press, 1992), argues that Churchill and Pam Gems are 'the two major women writers whose work has become an important and influential part of the general repertoire' (p. 452). However, he claims that this was achieved by the women dramatists 'distanc[ing] themselves from the radical and more

subjective side of the feminist movement' (ibid.), whereas I would argue that, in Churchill's case, it is the radicalism of her writing, both formally and ideologically, which has exceptionally secured her a place in the modern dramatic canon.

CHAPTER 3. THE DRAMATIST AS SOCIALIST CRITIC

1 Churchill, *Omnibus*, BBC1, November 1988.
2 Quoted in Thurman, *Ms.*, May 1982, 51–7; 54.
3 Ibid.
4 Churchill, *The Ants*, in *New English Dramatists*, vol. 12 (Harmondsworth: Penguin, 1969), 89–103; 103.
5 Ibid.
6 *Moving Clocks Go Slow* remains unpublished, but for a description and analysis of the play, see Kritzer, 1991, 67–72.
7 *Sunday Times*, 5 January 1975, 30.
8 For production photographs of the set, see *Plays and Players*, March 1975, 24–5.
9 Ibid., 25.
10 Hannah Arendt, *On Violence* (London: Penguin, 1970), 67.
11 *The Times*, 3 January 1975, 7.
12 Ibid.
13 *Sunday Times*, 5 January 1975, 7.
14 *Plays and Players*, March 1975, 25.
15 Ronald Hayman interview with Caryl Churchill and Max Stafford-Clark, *Sunday Times Magazine*, 2 March 1980, 25–7; 27.
16 Ibid.
17 In Rob Ritchie, (ed.), *The Joint Stock Book*, 119.
18 *Sunday Times Magazine*, 2 March 1980, 27.
19 *The Times*, 28 September 1976, 20.
20 *Plays and Players*, February 1977, 24.
21 Elin Diamond, 'Brechtian Theory / Feminist Theory', *The Drama Review*, vol. 32, no. 1 (Spring 1988), 82–94; 87.
22 Ibid.
23 Ibid.
24 *The Times*, 28 September 1976, 20.
25 Eva Figes, *Patriarchal Attitudes* (London: Virago, 1970, revised 1978), 9.
26 *The After-Dinner Joke* is published in *Churchill: Shorts* 165–221, and is a further example of the renewed topicality of Churchill's early work: charity as big business in our era of Live Aid, Comic Relief, and so on.
27 For details see Catherine Itzin, *Stages in the Revolution*, 280–1.

28 Lynne Truss interview, *Plays and Players*, January 1984, 10.
29 *Times Literary Supplement*, 20 January 1984, 62.
30 *New Statesman*, 27 January 1984, 30–1.
31 *Guardian*, 11 January 1984, 9.
32 On the crowd as performer, and the unpredictibility of crowd response, see Michel Foucault, *Discipline and Punish*, translated by Alan Sheridan (Harmondsworth: Penguin, 1977) 57–69.
33 Churchill underlined this point in her introduction to the play in 1985, when she commented 'as this edition goes to press, the Government are attempting to depoliticise the miners and the rioters by emphasising a "criminal element"' (P2 3).
34 Giles Gordon, *Spectator*, 21 January, 27–8; 28.
35 Foucault, *Discipline and Punish*, 25.
36 Ibid.
37 *Times Literary Supplement*, 20 January 1984, 62. For a production photograph of this scene, see Ros Asquith's review in *City Limits*, 20–26 January 1984, 48.
38 Jane Thomas, 'The Plays of Caryl Churchill: Essays in Refusal', in Adrian Page, (ed.), *The Death of the Playwright?* (Basingstoke: Macmillan, 1992), 160–85; 169–70.
39 Janelle Reinelt, *After Brecht* (Ann Arbor: University of Michigan Press, 1994), 96.

CHAPTER 4. COMMUNITIES IN DRAMATIC DIALOGUE

1 See Select Bibliography, 'Source material for plays', for details of sources relating to certain of the plays studied in this volume.
2 Mary Chamberlain, *Fenwomen: A Portrait of Women in an English Village* (1975; London: Routledge & Kegan Paul, 1983).
3 See Chamberlain, 112–14.
4 Ibid., 3.
5 Ibid., 2–3.
6 *Omnibus*, BBC1, November 1988.
7 Explained by the director of *Fen*, Les Waters, ibid.
8 *Plays and Players*, October 1983, 39–40; 40.
9 Liz Bale, 'Everyday Life', *Spare Rib*, July 1984, 50–3; 52.
10 Chamberlain, 11–12.
11 Beverly Hayne, *Sunday Times Magazine*, 24 July 1983, 31.
12 *Omnibus*, BBC1, November 1988.
13 Peter Lewis, *The Times*, 30 June 1987, 9.
14 Explained in the programme notes for the West End, Wyndham's production.
15 *The Times*, 30 June 1987, 9.

16 John Peter, *Sunday Times*, 29 March 1987, 51.
17 Janelle Reinelt, *After Brecht*, 97.
18 Churchill, 'Driven by Greed and Fear', *New Statesman*, 17 July 1987, 10–11; 10.
19 Clare Colvin, *Plays and Players*, May 1987, 14.
20 *The Times*, 30 June 1987, 9.
21 *The Times*, 7 July 1987, 18.
22 *The Times*, 30 June 1987, 9.
23 Ruby Cohn, *Retreats from Realism in Recent English Drama* (Cambridge: Cambridge University Press, 1991), 91.
24 *Serious Money* made £14,000 a week for the Royal Court, which generated the funds for the West End transfer to Wyndham's. See *The Times*, 30 June 1987, 9. It is *Cloud Nine*, however, which is reported to be Churchill's 'biggest earner'. See Claire Armistead, 'Tale of the Unexpected', *Guardian*, Section 2, Arts, 12 January 1994, 4–5; 5.
25 Details explained by Reva Klein in *Times Education Supplement*, 29 June 1990, 35.
26 Jim Hiley interview, *The Times*, 10 October 1990, 25
27 *The Times*, 26 June 1990, 18.
28 Janelle Reinelt, *After Brecht*, 103.
29 Jeremy Kingston, *The Times*, 11 October 1990, 26.
30 Ibid.
31 *The Times*, 10 October 1990, 25.

CHAPTER 5. EXPLODING WORDS AND WORLDS

1 Churchill, 'Not Ordinary, Not Safe: A Direction for Drama?', *Twentieth Century*, November 1960, 443–51; 446.
2 Ibid.
3 W. Stephen Gilbert, *Plays and Players*, March 1977, 33.
4 *The Times*, 28 January 1977, 9.
5 *Spare Rib*, October 1986, 33.
6 For details, see Fitzsimmons, *File on Churchill*, 68–70.
7 See Geraldine Cousin interview, *New Theatre Quarterly*, February 1988, 6.
8 Churchill, 'Legend of a Woman Possessed', *Guardian*, 21 November 1986, 17.
9 *Spare Rib*, October 1986, 33.
10 For a development of this point, see Elin Diamond, '(In)visible Bodies in Churchill's Theatre', 277–8.
11 Churchill had earlier developed the motif of a woman with the power of flight, the power to move objects in the unperformed

stage play *Seagulls* (1978), published in *Churchill: Shorts*, 223–43. In *Seagulls* it is the loss of this power which is dramatized as the central issue, and, as Churchill explains in the introduction to *Churchill: Shorts*, this made the play feel like 'it was about not being able to write for me to want it done at the time'.

12   Michel Foucault, introduction to *Herculine Barbin*, translated by Richard McDougall (New York: Pantheon, 1980), vii.

13   Ibid.

14   Irving Wardle, *The Times*, 28 November 1986, 13.

15   Ann Fitzgerald, *Plays and Players*, November 1986, 33.

16   *Guardian*, 29 November 1986, 14.

17   Michael Coveney noted that 'the pattern of the piece [*Icecream*] reminds me of earlier plays like *Traps* and *Owners*' (*Financial Times*, 12 April 1989, 23).

18   See commentary by Kevin Jackson, in interview with Churchill, *Independent*, 12 April 1989, 15.

19   Michael Coveney noted that this actually happened to 'the American director Alan Schneider at Hampstead Theatre a few years back', *Financial Times*, 12 April 1989, 23.

20   *The Times*, 12 April 1989, 21.

21   Kevin Jackson interview, *Independent*, 12 April 1989, 15.

22   Ibid.

23   Janelle G. Reinelt and Joseph R. Roach, (eds), *Critical Theory and Performance* (Ann Arbor: University of Michigan Press, 1992), 1.

24   Ibid.

25   Suzanne Moore, 'New Meanings for New Markets', *Women's Review*, April 1987, 26–7; 26.

26   *Independent*, 12 April 1989, 15.

27   *Guardian*, 11 April 1989, 45.

28   Ibid.

29   Churchill, *Independent*, 12 April 1989, 15.

30   For a further example of Churchill using film as an escape from reality, see her short 1980 play *Three More Sleepless Nights*, (S 245–73). In this drama, Pete's monosyllabic girlfriend, Dawn, commits suicide in their shared bed, while he escapes from their inability to communicate by relating movie narratives – in particular, episodes from the science fiction film *Aliens*.

31   Churchill, interview, *New Statesman and Society*, 21 April 1989, 41–2; 42.

32   See, for example, John Percival's review in *The Times*, (14 March 1991, 22), where he argues that production did not 'make up its mind what it is doing', and that potential lines of development were, in his view, 'lost in a morass of silly ideas and fancy theatrical posturing in different modes'. Generally, more favourable review-

ing came from dance critics. See, for example, Judith Mackrell's review, *Independent*, 16 March 1991, 32.

33 *Guardian*, 15 March 1991, 37.

34 Interview, *Late Theatre*, BBC2, January 1994.

35 Ibid.

36 For an explanation of the Kristevan semiotic, marginal and monumental, see my, *An Introduction to Feminism and Theatre*, 51–6.

37 Programme notes for *The Skriker* give explanations for the various different kinds of spirits. A thrumpin is explained as 'a kind of attendant demon, believed to haunt every man with the power of taking his life'; blue men 'wreck ships unless the captain can outwit them at rhyming games'.

38 Gwyn Morgan, *Plays and Players*, February 1994, 5.

39 See page 30 of the present study for related discussion of this issue in section on *Vinegar Tom*.

40 Explanations are from the programme notes to *The Skriker*.

41 *Late Theatre*, BBC2, January 1994.

42 I take the phrasing from Peggy Phelan's *Unmarked* (p. 19).

43 Paul Taylor, *Independent*, 29 January 1994, 52.

44 See Malcolm Rutherford's review, *Weekend Financial Times*, January 29–30, 1994, xxii.

45 *Late Theatre*, BBC2, January 1994.

46 Benedict Nightingale, *The Times*, 29 January 1994, 16.

47 *Late Theatre*, BBC2, January 1994.

48 Churchill, *Thyestes* (London: Nick Hern, 1995), xiii. In particular, the news was dominated by the internecine fighting and revenge killings in Rwanda.

49 Ibid.

50 'Flights of Fancy', *Independent*, Arts Section, 20 January 1994, 25.

CHAPTER 6. 1997 – *FAR AWAY*

1 David Benedict, *Independent*, Arts Section, 19 April 1997, 4.

2 Caryl Churchill, in Benedict interview, ibid.

3 Sheila Rabillard, ed., *Essays on Caryl Churchill: Contemporary Representations* (Winnipeg: Blizzard Publishing, 1998).

4 At the time of writing (January 2001), the cumulative MLA CD-rom index (which is never exhaustive) lists a dozen or so entries under Caryl Churchill for 1997 and after.

5 See Fiachra Gibbons, 'on the new relevance of Caryl Churchill's play *Light Shining in Buckinghamshire*', *Guardian*, 11 January 1997, 6.

6 Paul Foot, *Guardian*, 27 January 1997, 13.

7   For details of The Land Is Ours campaign, see 'Up in Smoke' by John Vidal and George Monbiot, *Guardian*, 16 October 1996, 1–3.

8   *The Times*, 22 March 1997, 23. *Cloud Nine*'s techniques of 'troubling gender' have been widely acknowledged in feminist theory and theatre (as discussed in Chap. 2), but for a contrasting view on this and an interrogation of *Cloud Nine*'s sexual radicalism see James M. Harding, 'Cloud Cover: (Re) Dressing Desire and Comfortable Subversions in Caryl Churchill's *Cloud Nine*', *Publications of the Modern Language Association*, 113: 2, March 1998, 258–72.

9   *Independent on Sunday*, Arts Section, 23 March 1997, 12.

10 *Independent*, Arts Section, 19 April 1997, 4.

11 My own criticism of The Old Vic revival of *Cloud Nine* was, in contrast to the excellent ensemble work of the *Light Shining* revival, the inability of Hall's company to develop and to sustain the collective style of performance required for the play.

12 Reviews appeared on 24 April 1997. On the 23rd April, the day after the opening of *Hotel*, reviewers were preoccupied with the revival of Brecht's *The Caucasian Chalk Circle* at the National.

13 *Guardian*, 24 April 1997, 2.

14 *Independent*, 24 April 1997, 19.

15 *The Times*, 24 April 1997, 37.

16 Daldry was appointed Artistic Director of the Royal Court in 1993, a position he held until 1998 when he became Director, then Associate Director. Under his directorship the Court began a major re-building project, funded primarily by National Lottery money and supplemented by private sponsorship and fund-raising. The company had to move out of Sloane Square during the re-building programme, and productions were staged either at the Duke of York's (Theatre Downstairs), or at the Ambassadors (Theatre Upstairs).

17 Jeremy Kingston, *The Times*, 2 July 1997, 34.

18 Quoted in Anna Day, 'Maximum Effort from *Blue Heart*', *The Sunday Times*, 24 August, 3.

19 Una Chaudhuri, *Staging Place: The Geography of Modern Drama* (Ann Arbor: University of Michigan Press, 1997), 130.

20 Frank Kermode, *The Sense of an Ending: Studies in the Theory of Fiction* Oxford: Oxford University Press, 1966), 47.

21 Ibid.

22 Elin Diamond, *Unmaking Mimesis* (London: Routledge, 1997), 100.

23 *The Sunday Times*, 31 August 1997, 14. While Peter praised *Blue Heart* as the highlight of the Edinburgh Fringe, other reviewers were less enthusiastic about the linguistic play in *Blue Kettle*. For example, see Neil Cooper, 'A Chinese puzzle and the new Caryl Churchill', *The Times*, 25 April 1997,16 and Bernard Levin, 'Kettle goes off the boil',

The Times, 1 October 1997, 32.

24 The Royal Court Theatre re-opened in Sloane Square in February 2000.

25 Rhoda Koenig, *Independent*, 2 December 2000, reproduced in *Theatre Record*, 18 November to 1 December 2000, 1575.

26 *Financial Times*, 4 December 2000, reproduced in *Theatre Record*, ibid., 1577.

27 *What's On*, 6 December 2000, reproduced in *Theatre Record*, ibid., 1574.

CHAPTER 7. A ROYAL COURT CELEBRATION

1 'David Hare, quoted in Royal Court publicity, 'Caryl Churchill Readings', 16–26 September 2008.

2 Mark Ravenhill, 'She Made Us Raise Our Game', *Guardian*, 3 September 2008, Arts Section, 23.

3 Churchill, *Identical Twins*, unpublished manuscript, 26.

4 In the original radio broadcast of *Identical Twins* both roles were played by Kenneth Haigh.

5 Dan Rebellato, ' "Because it feels fucking amazing": Recent British Drama and Bodily Mutilation', in Rebecca D'Monté and Graham Saunders (eds.), *Cool Britannia?: British Political Drama in the 1990s* (Basingstoke: Palgrave Macmillan, 2008), 192–207; 202.

6 See Sarah Franklin, 'Sheepwatching', *Anthropology Today*, Vol. 17, no. 3 (June 2001): 3–9. Explaining the famous cloning break through of Dolly the sheep, Franklin details the major discovery of scientist Ian Wilmut: the possibility that adult cells, once differentiated can, through the intervention of the cloning technique, be reversed, go back to a de-differentiated state, or possibly even that cells do not *'fully differentiate to begin with'* (emphasis in the original, 7).

7 Stephen Daldry, interview, in *A Number*, Royal Court Education Resources. Available online, http://www.royalcourttheatre.com/files/downloads/a_number_edupack.pdf.

8 See Sarah Franklin and Celia Roberts, *Born and Made: An Ethnography of Preimplantation Genetic Diagnosis* (Princeton: Princeton University Press, 2006), 2.

9 Heightening the sense of *A Number* as a family, father and son/s drama and further complicating ideas of familial resemblances was the casting of real life father and son, Timothy and Samuel West, in a revival of the play at the Crucible Theatre, Sheffield in 2006.

10 Hélène Cixous, in Cixous and Catherine Clément, trans. B. Wing, *The Newly Born Woman* (Manchester: Manchester University Press,

[1975], 1987), 79.

11 Jean Baudrillard, 'Clone Story', in *Simulacra and Simulation*, trans. S. F. Glaser (Ann Arbor: The University of Michigan Press, [1981], 1994), 95–103, 96–7.

12 Cixous, *The Newly Born Woman*, 79.

13 See note 6.

14 Preimplantation genetic diagnosis (PGD) has developed techniques that can help to screen embryos for genetic defects, but can also be used for genetic selection. For further details see Franklin and Roberts, *Born and Made*.

15 Franklin, 'Sheepwatching', 8.

16 John Peter, review of *A Number*, *Sunday Times*, 6 October 2002, reprinted in *Theatre Record*, 24 September–7 October 2002, 1278–9, 1279.

17 Stephen Daldry similarly describes the process of working on the text with performers as one of needing to 'understand what she's [Churchill] taken out' in order to get to grips with 'what Caryl has left in'. See *A Number*, Royal Court Education Resources.

18 Churchill had first seen Davies in 1979 in a performance of *The Seven Deadly Sins* and was drawn to the dancer's collaboration in this piece with singer-performer Julie Covington. Although Davies was one of the founding members of Second Stride, the company with whom Churchill was able to pursue her interdisciplinary performance collaborations (see Chapter 5), it was not until *Plants and Ghosts* in 2002 that Churchill and Davies had the opportunity to work together.

19 For a brief discussion of *A Dream Play* and comments from two members of the cast, see Philip Roberts, *About Churchill: the Playwright and the Work* (London: Faber & Faber, 2008), 155–6 and 265–6.

20 Churchill, *Caryl Churchill, Plays: 4* (London: Nick Hern Books, 2008), ix.

21 Ibid.

22 Jackie Stacey and Lynne Pearce (eds.), *Romance Revisited* (New York: New York University Press, 1995), introduction, 'The Heart of the Matter: Feminists Revisit Romance', 11–45, 16. This was also helpful in pointing me back to Roland Barthes's *A Lover's Discourse*, discussed further on in my chapter.

23 Sara Ahmed, *The Cultural Politics of Emotion* (Edinburgh: Edinburgh University Press, 2004), 130–1.

24 Ibid, 131.

25 Roland Barthes, *A Lover's Discourse*, trans. R. Howard (London: Jonathan Cape, 1979), 197–8.

26 Ibid, 97–8.

27 Churchill, *Plays 4*, vii–viii.

28 Ibid, viii.

29 Macdonald, in Roberts, *About Churchill*, 270.

30 Ibid, 271.

31 Macdonald explains how first of all 'we had to inform ourselves of the political background to the material – to know the argument as it were' (ibid, 270).

32 Ibid, 271.

33 A benefit performance of *Far Away* during its run at the Albery Theatre in 2001 was given for the Al Kasaba and Inad Palestinian theatres in the Occupied Territories. See Caryl Churchill, 'Theatre, West Bank Style', *Guardian* 21 February 2001. For further details of Churchill's support of Palestine and her involvement in other political protests, including her protest activities at the Court over the war in Iraq, see Philip Roberts, *About Churchill*, 155.

34 Churchill interview, 'The War on Gaza 2009', MAP, DVD (available through MAP, 33a Islington Park Street, London, N1 1Q8, UK).

35 *Seven Jewish Children* can be downloaded at http://www.nickhernbooks.co.uk/; http://www.royalcourttheatre.com/files/downloads/SevenJewishChildren.pdf; or http://casarotto.co.uk/uploads/File/SevenJewishChildren.pdf.

36 Mark Brown, 'Royal Court acts fast with Gaza crisis play', *Guardian*, 24 January 2009, UK news section, 16.

37 Ibid.

38 See for example Melanie Phillips, 'The Royal Court's Mystery Play', *Spectator*, 8 February 2009, http://www.spectator.co.uk/melanie phillips/3334851/the-royal-courts-mystery-play.thtml; Leon Symons, 'Outrage over "demonising" play for Gaza', *The Jewish Chronicle*, 12 February 2009, http://www.thejc.com/articles/outrage-over-demonising-play-gaza; Howard Jacobson 'Let's see the "criticism" of Israel for what it really is', *Independent*, 18 February 2009, 24–5; Martin Beckford, 'Prominent Jews accuse Royal Court play of demonising Israelis', http://www.telegraph.co.uk/culture/theatre/4691647/Prominent-Jews-accuse-Royal-Court-play-of-demonising-Israelis.html.

39 Churchill, 'My play is not anti-Semitic', reply to Howard Jacobson (see note 38), *Independent*, 21 February 2009, http://www.independent.co.uk/opinion/letters/letters-jacobson-on-gaza-1628191.html. For insightful defences of Churchill's play see Jacqueline Rose, 'Why Howard Jacobson is Wrong', *Guardian*, 24 February 2009 http://www.guardian.co.uk/commentisfree/2009/feb/23/howard-jacobson-antisemitism-caryl-churchill, and Tony Kushner and Alisa Solomon, 'Tell Her the Truth', *Nation*, 13 April 2009, http://www.thenation.com/doc/20090413/kushner_solomon.

40   See Ben Dowell, 'BBC rejects play on Israel's history for impartiality reasons', http://www.guardian.co.uk/media/2009/mar/16/bbc-rejects-caryl-churchill-israel.

41   http://www.guardian.co.uk/stage/video/2009/apr/25/seven-jewish-children-caryl-churchill.

42   In June 2009 a Hebrew translation of the play was performed in Tel Aviv, Israel through the auspices of the Coalition of Women for Peace, directed by the Palestinian political prisoner Samieh Jabbarin. For details see http://www.midnighteast.com/mag/?p=691, and http://www.guardian.co.uk/stage/2009/jun/12/caryl-churchill-seven-jewish-children-tel-aviv.

43   Churchill, *Independent*, 21 February 2009.

44   Churchill interview, 'The War on Gaza 2009', MAP, DVD.

45   Marius von Mayenburg, *The Stone*, (London: Methuen, 2009), 31.

46   Michael Billington, review of *Seven Jewish Children*, *Guardian*, 12 February 2009, 38.

47   The play can be performed by any number of performers in any space. As Churchill explains, the play:
     ...can be done by anyone, any where, with any number of people ...It could be read by one person. It could be read as a dialogue between two or three people...the scene is always domestic and quite simple and I think people should do it in whatever situation is appropriate for them. I mean it can be done in someone's living room, or it can be done in a hall, it can be in a theatre. It can be done any where at all. (Churchill interview, 'The War on Gaza 2009', MAP).

48   The script of *Seven Jewish Children* is not paginated. Numbers cited refer to the scenes.

49   Churchill's anti-Semitic accusers interpreted these lines as alluding to the blood libel against Jews. For Churchill's reply to this see *Independent*, 21 February 2009.

50   Churchill, *Independent*, 21 February 2009.

51   Churchill, quoted in Mark Brown, 'Royal Court acts fast with Gaza crisis play'.

Select Bibliography

PLAYS BY CHURCHILL

The Ants, in *New English Dramatists*, vol. 12, (Harmondsworth: Penguin, 1969), 89–103.

Churchill: Plays One – *Owners, Traps, Vinegar Tom, Light Shining in Buckinghamshire, Cloud Nine* (London: Methuen, 1985). Includes introduction and notes on individual plays by Churchill.

Objections to Sex and Violence, in *Plays by Women*, vol. 4 (London: Methuen, 1985), 11–53. Includes Afterword by Churchill.

A Mouthful of Birds, with David Lan (London: Methuen, 1986). Includes Churchill's notes on the workshop and the play.

Icecream (London: Nick Hern, 1989).

Churchill: Plays Two – *Softcops, Top Girls, Fen, Serious Money* (London: Methuen, 1990). Includes introduction and notes on individual plays by Churchill.

Churchill: Shorts – *Three More Sleepless Nights, Lovesick, The After-Dinner Joke, Abortive, Schreber's Nervous Illness, The Judge's Wife, The Hospital at the Time of the Revolution, Hot Fudge, Not Not Not Not Not Enough Oxygen, Seagulls* (London: Nick Hern, 1990). Includes introduction and notes on individual plays by Churchill.

Mad Forest (London: Nick Hern, 1990; revised 1991).

Lives of the Great Poisoners (London: Methuen, 1993). Production dossier with introductions by Churchill and principal collaborators.

The Skriker (London: Nick Hern, 1994).

Thyestes, Seneca, translated by Churchill (London: Nick Hern, 1995). Includes introduction detailing Churchill's approach to translation.

Hotel, with Second Stride (London: Nick Hern, 1997).

Churchill: Plays 3 (London: Nick Hern, 1998). Collection includes: *Icecream, Mad Forest, Thyestes, The Skriker, Lives of the Great Poisoners* and *A Mouthful of Birds* with David Lan. Introduction by Churchill.

Blue Heart (London: Nick Hern, 1997).

This is a Chair (London: Nick Hern, 1999).

Far Away (London: Nick Hern, 2000).

A Number (London: Nick Hern, 2002).

A Dream Play, August Strindberg, a new version by Churchill (London: Nick Hern, 2005).

Drunk Enough to Say I Love You? (London: Nick Hern, 2006).

Caryl Churchill: Plays 4 (London: Nick Hern, 2008). Includes: *Hotel, This is a Chair, Blue Heart, Far Away, A Number, A Dream Play* and *Drunk Enough to Say I Love You?* Introduction by Churchill.

Seven Jewish Children (London: Nick Hern, 2009).

SOURCE MATERIAL FOR PLAYS

Sources which Churchill identifies as influencing, or indeed directly shaping her theatre, offer excellent ways into both academic study and practical exploration of her work. The following is a list of a number of the plays, together with some sources of background material.

Cloud Nine
Fanon, Frantz, *Black Skin, White Masks,* (New York: Grove Press, 1967). On colonialism.

Genet, Jean. His theatre, for colonialism and gender oppression.

Millett, Kate, *Sexual Politics* (1970; London: Virago, 1977).

Fen
Chamberlain, Mary, *Fenwomen: A Portrait of Women in an English Village* (1975; London: Routledge & Kegan Paul, 1983).

The Hospital at the Time of the Revolution
Fanon, Frantz, *The Wretched of the Earth,* translated by Constance Farrington (Harmondsworth: Penguin, 1967). On colonialism.

Laing, R. D., *The Divided Self* (1960; Harmondsworth: Penguin/Pelican, 1965). On schizophrenia.

Light Shining in Buckinghamshire
Churchill, Caryl, *Plays One,* p. 189, gives a list of documentary materials used in the play.

Lives of the Great Poisoners
Stokes, Hugh, *Mme de Brinvilliers and Her Times, 1630–1676* (London: John Lane, 1912), and see Churchill, *Lives of the Great Poisoners,* p. ix, for details of epistolary material consulted.

A Mouthful of Birds
Euripides, *The Bacchae* (Harmondsworth: Penguin, 1954).

McDougall, Richard, translator, *Herculine Barbin: Being the Recently Discovered Memoirs of a Nineteenth-Century French Hermaphrodite*, with introduction by Michel Foucault (New York: Pantheon Books, 1980).

Objections to Sex and Violence
Arendt, Hannah, *On Violence* (London: Penguin, 1970).

Owners
Figes, Eva, *Patriarchal Attitudes* (1970, London: Faber & Faber, 1978). On women's oppression.

Schreber's Nervous Illness
Schreber, Daniel Paul, *Memoirs of My Nervous Illness*, edited and translated by Ida Macalpine and Richard A. Hunter (London: William Dawson & Sons, 1955).

Serious Money
Shadwell, Thomas, *The Volunteers, or the Stock-Jobbers* (London, 1693).

The Skriker
Briggs, Mary Katharine, *The Fairies in Tradition and Literature* (London: Routledge & Kegan Paul, 1967). On folklore and folktales.

Softcops
Foucault, Michel, *Discipline and Punish*, translated by Alan Sheridan (Harmondsworth: Penguin, 1977).

Top Girls
Barr, Pat, *A Curious Life for a Lady* (London: Secker & Warburg, 1970). On Isabella Bird.
Brazell, Karen, translator, *The Confessions of Lady Nijo* (New York: Anchor Books, 1973). On Lady Nijo.

Vinegar Tom
Ehrenreich, Barbara, and Deidre English, *Witches, Midwives and Nurses* (New York: Feminist Press, 1973). On witchcraft and women as healers.

Drunk Enough to Say I Love You?
Blum, William, *Killing Hope: U.S. Military and CIA Interventions Since World War II* (Monroe, Me.: Common Courage, 1995).
——— *Rogue State: A Guide to the World's Only Super Power* (Monroe, Me.: Common Courage, 2000).

INTERVIEWS

Benedict, David, 'The Mother of Reinvention', arts section, *Independent*,

19 April 1997, 4. Includes discussion of revival of Light Shining and Cloud Nine, and original working methods with Joint Stock.

Betsko, Kathleen and Rachel Koenig (eds), 'Caryl Churchill', *Interviews with Contemporary Women Playwrights* (New York: Beech Tree Books, 1987), 75–84. Has detail on *Top Girls, Fen, Cloud Nine* and working method with Joint Stock.

Cousin, Geraldine, 'The Common Imagination and the Individual Voice', *New Theatre Quarterly*, vol. IV, no. 13, February 1988, 3–16. Churchill talks about her career and plays. Discusses *A Mouthful of Birds* and *Serious Money* in detail.

Gooch, Steve, 'Caryl Churchill, author of this month's playtext, talks to p & p', *Plays and Players*, January 1973, 40, and p. 1 of script inset (the issue contains the complete script of *Owners*). Mainly about *Owners*.

Gussow, Mel, 'Caryl Churchill: A Genteel Playwright with an Angry Voice', *New York Times*, 22 November 1987, 1, 26. Interview during run of *Serious Money*.

Hayman, Ronald, 'Partners: Caryl Churchill and Max Stafford-Clark', *Sunday Times Magazine*, 2 March 1980, 25–7. On workshopping with Joint Stock.

Hiley, Jim, 'Revolution in Miniature', *The Times*, 10 October 1990, 25. Churchill talks about *Mad Forest*.

Jackson, Kevin, 'Incompatible Flavours', *Independent*, 12 April 1989, 15. On *Icecream*.

Kay, Jackie, 'Interview with Caryl Churchill', *New Statesman and Society*, 21 April 1989, 41–2. Churchill talks about her career in the theatre, audience reactions to *Serious Money*, and the production of *Icecream*.

Late Theatre, 'Interview with Churchill', BBC2, broadcast January 1994. Churchill talks about the production of *The Skriker*. Includes footage of *The Skriker* in rehearsal.

McFerran, Ann, 'The Theatre's (Somewhat) Angry Young Women', *Time Out*, 28 October–3 November 1977, 13–15. Discussion with contemporary women playwrights including Churchill.

Mackrell, Judith, 'Flights of Fancy', *Independent*, 20 January 1994, 25. Interview during rehearsal of *The Skriker*.

MAP, Churchill interview, 'War on Gaza 2009', DVD. Churchill contexualizes *Seven Jewish Children* as 'a play for Gaza'.

Omnibus on Caryl Churchill, BBC1, broadcast November 1988. Excellent documentary combining interview footage with performed extracts by Joint Stock/Royal Court players.

Simon, John, 'Sex, Politics, and Other Play Things', *Vogue*, August 1983, 126, 130. Includes discussion of *Top Girls, Fen* and workshopping of *Cloud Nine*.

Truss, Lynne, 'A Fair Cop', *Plays and Players*, January 1984, 8–10. Details *Softcops*.

Winer, Laurie, 'Caryl Churchill, Ex-Idealogue, Trusts to Luck', *New York Times*, 29 April 1990. On Churchill's dislike of interviews and *Icecream*.

STUDIES OF CHURCHILL'S WORK

Full-Length Studies

Aston, Elaine and Diamond, Elin (eds.), *The Cambridge Companion to Caryl Churchill* (Cambridge: Cambridge University Press, 2009). Collection of new scholarship on Churchill's theatre.

Cousin, Geraldine, *Churchill The Playwright* (London: Methuen, 1989). Very descriptive approach. Useful for plot summaries of early unpublished work.

Fitzsimmons, Linda (compiler), *File on Churchill* (London: Methuen, 1989). Contains synopses of plays and review material.

Kritzer, Amelia Howe, *The Plays of Caryl Churchill: Theatre of Empowerment* (Basingstoke: Macmillan, 1991). Detailed study which makes good use of critical theory and criticism to frame analysis.

Rabillard, Sheila (ed.), *Essays on Caryl Churchill: Contemporary Representations* (Winnipeg: Blizzard Publishing, 1998). Includes essays on the 1991 revival of *Top Girls*, *The Skriker*, and a very good account by Susan Bennett on different productions of *Cloud Nine*.

Randall, Phyllis R. (ed.), *Caryl Churchill: A Casebook* (London and New York: Garland, 1988). Useful to dip in to. Bibliography offers explanatory framings for further reading suggestions.

Roberts, Philip, *About Churchill: the Playwright and the Work* (London: Faber & Faber, 2008). Includes detailed commentaries on plays, including unpublished early work and has a section for 'Voices and Documents' with interviews and materials from Churchill's collaborators which is an excellent resource.

Tycer, Alicia, *Caryl Churchill's Top Girls* (London and New York: Continuum, 2008). Includes detailed contextualization on the play, and ideas for workshops.

Essays and Articles

Amich, Candice, 'Bringing the Global Home: The Commitment to Caryl Churchill's *The Skriker*', *Modern Drama* 50.3, Fall 2007, 394–413.

Armitstead, Claire, 'Tale of the Unexpected', *Guardian*, Section 2, Arts, 12 January 1994, 4–5. Article written while *The Skriker* in rehearsal. Looks back over Churchill's career and profiles her current interest in dance-drama work. Some direct quotation of Churchill included.

Aston, Elaine, 'Telling Feminist Tales: Caryl Churchill', in *Feminist Views on the English Stage* (Cambridge: Cambridge University Press, 2003), 18–36. On Churchill's theatre in the 1990s.

————' "A Licence to Kill": Caryl Churchill's Socialist-Feminist "Ideas of Nature"' in Gabriella Giannachi and Nigel Stewart, (eds.), *Performing Nature: Explorations in Ecology and the Arts* (Bern: Peter Lang, 2005), 165–78. A discussion of Churchill's ecological concerns from *Not...Enough Oxygen* to *Far Away*.

Barnett, Claudia, ' "Reveangance Is Gold Mine, Sweet": Alchemy and Archetypes in Caryl Churchill's *The Skriker*'. *Essays in Theatre/Etudes Théâtrales* 19:1, 2000, 45–57.

Bazin, Victoria, ' "[Not] Talking 'Bout My Generation": Historicizing Feminisms in Caryl Churchill's *Top Girls*', *Studies in the Literary Imagination*, 39:2, Fall 2006, 115–34.

Benedict, David, with Linda Bassett, Graham Cowley, Deborah Findlay and Rick Fisher, 'Reputations: Caryl Churchill', *Theatre Voices*, 8 April 2005, http://www.theatrevoice.com/thearchive/. Excellent roundtable discussion of Churchill's work by practitioners involved in productions of her plays.

Burk, Julie Thompson, 'Top Girls and the Politics of Representation', in Ellen Donkin and Susan Clement (eds), *Upstaging Big Daddy: Directing Theater as if Gender and Race Matter* (Ann Arbor: University of Michigan Press, 1993), 67–78. On directing a production of *Top Girls*.

Carlson, Susan, 'Comic Collisions: Convention, Rage, and Order', *New Theatre Quarterly*, vol. 3, no. 12, November 1987, 303–16. Has section on Churchill's play with comic conventions in *Cloud Nine*.

Chambers, Colin, and Mike Prior, 'Caryl Churchill: Women and the Jigsaw of Time', in *Playwrights' Progress: Patterns of Postwar British Drama* (Oxford: Amber Lane Press, 1987), 189–98. Surveys Churchill's career in context of male-dominated tradition of British drama.

Churchill, Caryl, 'Not Ordinary, Not Safe: A Direction for Drama?', *The Twentieth Century*, November 1960, 443–51.

———— 'Driven By Greed and Fear', *New Statesman*, 17 July 1987, 10–11. Churchill on the City and *Serious Money*.

———— on workshopping *Light Shining in Buckinghamshire* in, Ritchie, 118–21.

Cornish, Roger, and Violet Ketels (eds), 'Caryl Churchill' in *Landmarks of Modern British Drama: The Plays of the Seventies* (London: Methuen, 1986, 525–31). Survey and introduction to *Top Girls* (also published in the volume).

Diamond, Elin, '(In)Visible Bodies in Churchill's Theater', in Lynda Hart (ed.), *Making a Spectacle: Feminist Essays on Contemporary Women's Theatre* (Ann Arbor: University of Michigan Press, 1989), 259–81. Excellent theoretically informed essay which looks at the body and issues of representation, detailing *Fen* and *A Mouthful of Birds*.

———— 'Refusing the Romanticism of Identity: Narrative Interventions in Churchill, Benmussa, Duras', in Sue-Ellen Case (ed.), *Performing Feminisms: Feminist Critical Theory and Theatre* (London and Baltimore: Johns Hopkins University Press, 1990), 92–105. Details *Cloud Nine* in context of representation and issues of gender and history.

———— 'Caryl Churchill's Plays: the *Gestus* of Invisibility', in *Unmaking Mimesis* (London: Routledge, 1997), 83–100. A development of '(In)Visible Bodies in Churchill's Theatre'. Includes brief note on *The Skriker*.

———— 'Caryl Churchill: Feeling Global', in Mary Luckhurst (ed.), *A Companion to Modern British and Irish Drama 1880–2005* (Oxford: Blackwell, 2006), 476–87. Excellent analysis of Churchill's long-standing concern with the dramatization of capitalist critique and 'mental states'.

Dymkowski, Christine, 'Caryl Churchill: *Far Away*...but Close to Home', *European Journal of English Studies*, 7:1, 2003, 55–68.

Edwardes, Jane, 'Celebrating Caryl Churchill', *Time Out*, 14 November 2006, http://www.timeout.com/london/theatre/features/2259.html. Edwardes interviews playwrights April de Angelis, Stella Feehily and Laura Wade about the significance of Churchill's theatre.

Evan, Raima, 'Women and Violence in *A Mouthful of Birds*', *Theatre Journal*, 54:2, May 2002, 263–84.

Fitzsimmons, Linda, 'I won't turn back for you or anyone: Caryl Churchill's Socialist-Feminist Theatre', *Essays in Theatre*, vol. 6, no. 1 (November 1987), 19–29. Examines *Top Girls* and *Fen* as political drama, specifically socialist-feminist drama.

Hanna, Gillian, *Feminism and Theatre*, Theatre Papers, 2nd series, no. 8 (Dartington, Devon: Dartington College, 1978). Discusses Monstrous Regiment's production of *Vinegar Tom*.

Harding, James, M., 'Cloud Cover: (Re)Dressing Desire and Comfortable Subversions in Caryl Churchill's *Cloud Nine*, *PMLA*, 113:2, March 1998, 258–272. Argues that *Cloud Nine* reasserts rather than challenges liberal ideology. A provocative contrast to the body of feminist work on this play.

Innes, Christopher, 'Caryl Churchill: Theatre as a Model for Change', in *Modern British Drama 1890–1990* (Cambridge: Cambridge University Press, 1992), 460–72. Survey-style essay.

Itzin, Catherine, 'Caryl Churchill', in *Stages in the Revolution* (London: Methuen, 1980), 279–87. Combines brief biographical detail with commentary on early work. Useful detail with regard to *The Legion Hall Bombing* broadcast and the censorship issue.

Jernigan, Daniel, '*Traps, Softcops, Blue Heart* and *This is a Chair*: Tracking Epistemological Upheaval in Caryl Churchill's Shorter Plays', *Modern Drama*, 47:1, 2004, 21–43.

——— 'Serious Money Becomes "Business by Other Means": Caryl Churchill's Metatheatrical Subject', Comparative Drama, 38:2–3, 2004, 291–313.

Jung, Woomin, 'Reading of a Post-Modern Feministic Body in The Skriker', Journal of Modern British and American Drama, 71:3, 2004, 181–208.

Keyssar, Helene, 'The Dramas of Caryl Churchill: the Politics of Possibility', in Feminist Theatre (Basingstoke: Macmillan, 1984), 77–101. Descriptive chapter on Churchill's plays.

Kintz, Linda, 'Performing Capital in Caryl Churchill's Serious Money', Theatre Journal, 51:3, 1999, 251–65.

Kushner, Tony and Solomon, Alisa, 'Tell Her the Truth', The Nation, 26 March 2009. Excellent and eloquent defence of Seven Jewish Children.

Lavell, Iris, 'Caryl Churchill's The Hospital at the time of the Revolution', Modern Drama, 45:1, Spring 2002, 76–94.

Mairowitz, David Zane, 'God and the Devil', Plays and Players, February 1977, 24–5. Review article assessing Light Shining in Buckinghamshire and Vinegar Tom.

Marohl, Joseph, 'De-realised Women: Performance and Identity in Top Girls', Modern Drama, vol. 30, no. 3 (September 1987), 376–88. Frames Top Girls in context of gender and issues of representation.

Mitchell, Tony, 'Caryl Churchill's Mad Forest: Polyphonic Representations of Southeastern Europe', Modern Drama, 36:4, December 1993, 499–511.

Pocock, Stephanie, '"God's in this Apple": Eating and Spirituality in Churchill's Light Shining in Buckinghamshire', Modern Drama, 50.1, Spring 2007, 60–76.

Quigley, Austin E., 'Stereotype and Prototype: Character in the Plays of Caryl Churchill', in Enoch Brater (ed.), Feminine Focus (Oxford: Oxford University Press, 1989), 25–52. Examines character in context of Churchill's 'social radicalism' and 'theatrical innovation'.

Rabillard, Sheila, 'Churchill's Fen and the Production of a Feminist Ecotheatre', Theater 25.1, 1994, 62–71.

Ravenhill, Mark, 'She Made Us Raise Our Game', Guardian, arts section, 3 September 2008, 23. Assesses Churchill's influence on contemporary playwrights.

Rebellato, Dan, 'The Personal Is Not Political: Caryl Churchill's Drunk Enough to Say I Love You?', Western European Stages, 19.1, Winter 2007, 33–6.

Reinelt, Janelle, 'Beyond Brecht: Britain's New Feminist Drama', in Performing Feminisms, 150–9. Has detail on Vinegar Tom and Monstrous Regiment.

——— 'Caryl Churchill: Socialist Feminism and Brechtian Dramaturgy', in After Brecht: British Epic Theater (Ann Arbor: University of

Michigan Press, 1994), 81–107. Excellent study of Churchill as 'one of Brecht's successors'. Teases out complexities and tensions of Brecht and feminism.

—— Caryl Churchill and the Politics of Style' in Elaine Aston and Janelle Reinelt (eds.), *The Cambridge Companion to Modern British Women Playwrights* (Cambridge: Cambridge University Press, 2000), 174–193. An insightful contextualizing essay that situates Churchill's early and later work in its socio-cultural milieu.

Ritchie, Rob (ed.), *The Joint Stock Book: The Making of a Theatre Collective* (London: Methuen, 1987). Has sections on *Light Shining in Buckinghamshire*, *Cloud Nine* and *Fen*.

Roberts, Philip and Stafford-Clark, Max, 'Case Study of *Cloud Nine*' and 'Case Study of *Serious Money*', in *Taking Stock: The Theatre of Max Stafford-Clark* (London: Nick Hern, 2007), 68–96; 124–46. Illuminating insights from Stafford-Clark and others on the working processes and first productions of these plays.

Rose, Jacqueline, 'Why Howard Jacobson is Wrong', *Guardian*, 24 February 2009. Defending *Seven Jewish Children* against accusations of anti-Semitism.

Sher, Tony, on workshopping *Cloud Nine*, in Ritchie, 138–42.

Solomon, Alisa, 'Witches, Ranters and the Middle Class: The Plays of Caryl Churchill', *Theater*, vol. 12, no. 2 (1981), 49–55. Details *Owners*, *Vinegar Tom* and *Light Shining in Buckinghamshire*.

Spink, Ian, 'Collaborations', in *Border Tensions: Dance and Discourse, Proceedings of the Fifth Study of Dance Conference*, Department of Dance Studies: University of Surrey, 1995, 293–302. Spink discusses his collaborations with Churchill including *A Mouthful of Birds*, *Fugue*, *Lives of the Great Poisoners* and *The Skriker*.

Stoller, Jennie, on *Fen*, in Ritchie, 150–52.

Swanson, Michael, 'Mother/Daughter Relationships in Three Plays by Caryl Churchill', *Theatre Studies*, 31 (1986), 49–66. Covers *Cloud Nine*, *Top Girls* and *Fen*.

Thomas, Jane, 'The Plays of Caryl Churchill: Essays in Refusal', in Adrian Page (ed.), *The Death of the Playwright?* (Basingstoke: Macmillan, 1992), 160–85. Useful, albeit literary, reading of Churchill through Foucault. Details *Softcops*, *Cloud Nine* and *Top Girls*.

Thurman, Judith, 'The Playwright Who Makes You Laugh About Orgasm, Racism, Class Struggle, Homophobia, Woman-Hating, the British Empire, and the Irrepressible Strangeness of the Human Heart', *Ms.*, May 1982, 51, 54, 57. Surveys Churchill's career and details *Cloud Nine*. Also has interview input from Churchill.

Varty, Anne, 'From Queens to Convicts: Status, Sex and Language in Contemporary British Women's Drama', *Essays and Studies*, 47 (1994), 65–89. Has brief commentary on language and power in *Top Girls* and *Serious Money*.

Wandor, Michelene, 'Free Collective Bargaining', *Time Out*, 30 March–5 April 1979, 14–16. Details workshopping and rehearsal processes of *Cloud Nine*.

—— 'Existential Women: *Owners* and *Top Girls*', in *Look Back in Gender: Sexuality and the Family in Post-War British Drama* (London: Methuen, 1987), 119–25. Brief analysis of domesticity and work in the two plays.

Yi, Jina, 'Envisioning Identities: Political and Theatrical Innovations in Caryl Churchill's *Top Girls*', *Journal of Modern British and American Drama* 18:1, 2005, 141–68.

OTHER RELEVANT MATERIAL

Aston, Elaine, *An Introduction to Feminism and Theatre* (London: Routledge, 1995).

—— (ed.), *Feminist Theatre Voices: A Collective Oral History* (Loughborough: Loughborough Theatre Texts, 1997).

Case, Sue-Ellen, *Feminism and Theatre* (Basingstoke: Macmillan, 1988).

—— and Jeanie K. Forte, 'From Formalism to Feminism', *Theater*, 16 (1985), 62–5.

Chesler, Phyllis, *Sacred Bond: Motherhood Under Siege* (London: Virago, 1990).

Cixous, Hélène, 'The Laugh of the Medusa', in Elaine Marks and Isabelle de Courtivron (eds), *New French Feminisms* (Brighton: Harvester, 1981), 245–64.

—— and Catherine Clément, *The Newly Born Woman* (Manchester: Manchester University Press, 1987).

Cohn, Ruby, *Retreats from Realism in Recent English Drama* (Cambridge: Cambridge University Press, 1991).

Diamond, Elin, 'Brechtian Theory / Feminist Theory', *The Drama Review*, vol. 32, no. 1 (Spring 1988), 82–94.

Ellman, Maud, *The Hunger Artists* (London: Virago, 1993).

Faludi, Susan, *Backlash* (London: Vintage, 1991 and 1992).

Grosz, Elizabeth, *Volatile Bodies: Toward a Corporeal Feminism* (Bloomington and Indianapolis: Indiana University Press, 1994).

Hanna, Gillian (compiler), *Monstrous Regiment: A Collective Celebration* (London: Nick Hern, 1991).

Moi, Toril, *Sexual/Textual Politics: Feminist Literary Theory* (London: Routledge, 1985).

Moore, Suzanne, 'New Meanings for New Markets', *Women's Review*, April 1987, 26–7.

Phelan, Peggy, *Unmarked: The Politics of Performance* (London: Routledge, 1993).

Reinelt, Janelle G., and Joseph Roach (eds), *Critical Theory and Performance* (Ann Arbor: University of Michigan Press, 1992).

Showalter, Elaine, *The Female Malady* (London: Virago, 1987).

Index